FINDING MY WAY

Sarah Houston

ISBN 979-8-9941144-0-7

Contact: sarahhoustonauthor@gmail.net

Traveler, there is no road. You make your own
path as you walk.   —Antonio Machado

CONTENTS

PREFACE

This memoir is a wide-ranging journey through a number of significant occurrences in my life, some involving my sixth sense. These are nestled among accounts of my growing up on a farm in Vermont and my life as a wife, mother, and later "hugger," a term for live-in partner in a Maine fishing village where I lived for a time.

Lots of people — even many I've known for a long time — don't really know me. I was painfully shy as a child. I am less so now, but have always had a voice that many people couldn't hear very well. Not being lightning-quick to know what I think and put it into words, I am often upstaged, outrun, or overridden by faster, louder, more verbal folks in classrooms, meetings, and gatherings. The irony is that in writing about myself so others will know me I find myself staring into a mirror and seeing myself in a fuller, more dimensional way. It has to do with remembering and reliving many experiences in the course of writing about them — perhaps a reason for writing a memoir in the first place.

To quite an extent my life has been enhanced by forces beyond rational explanation. Beginning when I was eleven and discovered that I could find water underground by wielding a forked stick, i.e. dowsing, I have used this ability for not only locating water, but also for self-healing, where best to plant a tree, and how to get myself "unlost." Over time, I've come to rely on this "sixth sense" for other things such as which supplements to take, spices to use in cooking, color choices for home décor, and knowing that my son was safe when worried because I was unable to reach him.

I've come to understand that while many people do not share this avenue of knowing, a number of people do; some of them more adeptly than I. Like musical ability, facility with math, and many other aptitudes, I understand it as something one is born with and, as is the case with so many things, we tend to use what we are good at.

Over the years dowsing has saved me from some rather fraught situations. Although I've never particularly subscribed to the idea that we have spirit guides, on occasion it has indeed felt as though certain opportunities and coincidences bore the hallmark of divine intervention. I hasten to add that this has not been the case all of the time, and I know there are people who are not part of the dowsing community who also experience this same phenomenon.

When I began writing these essays, they were standalones perhaps headed for local periodicals. Then it occurred to me to string them together for a memoir. As I proceeded to write them in loosely chronological order while keeping in mind my experiences with sixth-sense phenomena as a theme, I thought I should include something about my early years growing up on a farm. When it was suggested that intimate hands-on accounts of farm life in the 40s and 50s might be novel and engaging to others given how vastly different dairy farming has become, I expanded on this theme as well.

I couldn't imagine writing about my life without including some of my seminal experiences as a seeker which occurred in workshops and programs over many years. These included the three-year Extension of Human Capacities program that I attended with Jean Houston and Robert Masters at the helm, as well as eight 40-day Ark trainings created by Bill Smukler.

Jean Houston is a scholar, philosopher, and researcher in the Human Potential Movement. A psychologist, Bill Smukler designed and led 40-day psychological intensives, which provided a multimodal psychotherapeutic experience for some twelve to twenty trainees on each Ark plus training for those in the group desiring to become therapists or to enhance their practices.

At a dinner in recent times with all five of my sisters present, Amy floated the question: "What do you regret?"

I considered the query. There are many little things I wish I had said or not said, done or not done, but they were not consequential. As for bigger things, I don't regret my marriage to Jack; it was very good for a time, and we co-parented well before and after we separated. One thing I do wish I had done differently is provide a more consistent home and school environment for my son Jeremiah while he was growing up. I didn't think about it at the time, but attending four different schools from sixth grade through high school has to have been difficult. However, he appears to be doing just fine despite the vagaries of home and school life during those years and maintains that on balance his experience was positive.

Writing has been a life-long theme for me. When I was 10, I entered a story-writing contest in The Country Gentleman, a magazine focused on farming and rural life. The monthly had a section for the farmer's wife and something called "The Hodge Podge Page" for children. My little story won.

In addition to writing up the meetings for our 4-H club when I was twelve, having my stories appear in The Wick, my high school literary publication, reporting for The Worcester Telegram and Gazette, The Boston Herald and later, weeklies in Vermont, I also led writing groups in Pacific Palisades, California, and more recently as part of my therapeutic practice at Wellspring in Hardwick.

I did some "automatic writing" after reading a book by William Blake on the subject and included many of the poems I wrote in this vein in a booklet of poetry that I put together. I had a play published in Plays magazine, and some of my early poems were included in a League of Vermont Writers anthology. A few years ago I self-published The Quiet One, a slim novel for children.

I think I didn't really have a perspective on my life while I was pell-mell in the midst of living it; it was only later in a quieter time that I could see where I had been.

1. VISIT FROM A DOWSER

It was mild for May that Saturday in 1949—just a few fluffy clouds drifting across a blue sky. Bees buzzed in the dandelions, violets, and in our cherry tree still in bloom. I was about to be introduced to dowsing using a forked stick for finding underground water.

The dowser arrived at our farm in Walden soon after my father and grandfather came in from the morning milking, and were just finishing breakfast—oatmeal with maple syrup and cream and hot-from-the-oven graham rolls. The rest of us were also seated around the table: my mother in a flowered apron, her chestnut hair rolled back from her face; me in pigtails, age eleven, and my siblings: wavy-haired Sue, eight; Amy and Judy, five and four, chubby and bug-eyed as they took in the stranger. In those days whenever someone came to our house, which was five miles from the nearest town, it was an event., My brother Gary was two, and Anne was in the highchair with food on her face, her fists, and her hair.

After pleasantries and coffee, the visitor, balding and slight in slacks and a windbreaker, got his dowsing rod from his car.

"Cherry," he says, holding up a small forked stick. He is a man of few words. He and my rugged, 6-foot-2 dad in denim and flannel, my mustached grandfather in his bib-overalls, and tag-along me in jeans and a striped tee, set out to find underground water veins.

Off we trek to the upper fields, my father and grandfather chatting amiably, the dowser responding now and then with a grunt, and me keeping up so as not to miss anything. When we arrive at the area where my father hopes to find water, the man demonstrates technique. Grasping the wings of the switch firmly in his hands, the V pointing away from his body and parallel to the ground, he takes a few measured steps. Standing perfectly still we watch intently as the tip of his rod slowly and steadily dips downward.

"Water under here," he says.

My father shakes his head. Hard to believe. Then he tries it, holding the stick in his big hands and moving forward just as the dowser had.

Nothing happens. The switch point does not move.

My grandfather gives it a go. Same V-shaped rod, same measured pace. Again, it does not move.

Then it's my turn. I hold the wings tightly in a fine tension and take a few steps. We all watch as the tip steadily dips downward as I move forward. Seemingly of its own accord, it points to the ground.

A thrill spirals up from my belly, ending in a big smile. It worked! I found water using a cherry stick!

My father and grandfather both try again, but no dice. As we walk slowly back to the house in the sunshine I feel bigger, stronger, and lighter somehow. And though they don't say very much I can tell my father is pleased, maybe even a little proud of me.

Finding water with a dowsing rod was to be the first of many seemingly inexplicable experiences I have had over the years; incidents that lay outside the laws of physics or at least beyond my understanding of how things work. Eventually, I was to discover that dowsing could be used for more sophisticated objectives; illnesses could be diagnosed, remedies for ailments discovered, and missing objects or people located (the first lost person I found was myself when I was able to get *unlost* one time using this same process).

There was always an aura of mystery around these occurrences, which seemed at once magical and ordinary. They have rescued me on occasion, opened the way to finding healing and remedies, and have made my life better and more interesting in countless small ways over the years.

2. CHILDHOOD

My childhood was not unlike that of many other farm kids in the 40s and 50s — large family, a grandparent or two in the household, chores beginning at an early age, and a vast outdoor playground.

I wasn't aware of the ups and downs of the economy in those days, but felt them on a visceral level; my body would contract when my father said we were going to have to "tighten our belts," probably in response to a drop in the price paid for milk, the cost of grain going up, or radio newscasters warning of hard times ahead.

Since my father and his brother Jody operated the farm together with my grandfather in my early years, I had cousins living close by. They were near in age to me and my sisters, and we played together every day.

One time, my cousins, Ruthie, Shirley, and Thelma, and my sister Sue and I were rag-taggling through the day doing whatever presented itself when we noticed Old Pet in the barnyard, drowsing in the sun and chewing her cud. Her big brown presence beckoned us. Although we had Ayrshires, Jerseys, a couple of Guernseys, and three Holsteins, this one Brown Swiss was our favorite because she was always calm, gentle and friendly. We would sometimes give her extra handfuls of grain from the wheelbarrow on the feed floor though my father never doled out grain except for when the cows were about to be milked.

I forget who suggested we climb onto her back like you would a horse. She stood perfectly still as Sue petted her and my cousin Ruthie helped me up. Surprisingly, she didn't buck or run or seem to mind in the least; she just stood there. I urged her to move pommeling her ribs with my bare heels, but she didn't seem to understand. A horse would know you wanted it to take you somewhere.

We took turns, each of us getting up there, but even though we said *giddyup* and pressed her to move forward, Old Pet stood stock still. Didn't move an inch.

Another fun thing we did took place in St. Johnsbury. My family went there once or twice a month for groceries and other shopping, and my sisters and I often found our way to The Fairbanks Museum of Natural History where two magnificent bronze lions guarded the entrance. We'd climb all over those great creatures and dare one another to put a hand into one of those open mouths with its big teeth. When someone did, we all shrieked and the hand was hastily removed.

In point of fact, those sculpted bronze lions never once bit anyone, but it was great fun to scare ourselves pretending they would.

Like children everywhere, who have the time and space and perhaps other kids to play with, we created our own fun. Inventiveness was not only allowed, but was fostered. One day when I was about nine I told my mother I wanted to bake something that had never been made before — that I didn't want to follow any recipe. She set me up with a bowl in which I mixed some combination of flour, salt, leavening agent, an egg, and milk, which I put in a greased pan and baked. It tasted strange, but the process of "inventing it" was enormously satisfying.

3. I LEARN A NEW SKILL

I was five when I began filling the wood box. At age ten I graduated to feeding the calves. My father showed me how to put two fingers inside the new calf's mouth, which was warm and soft and wet—no teeth yet. He told me to spread my fingers apart so that when I brought the calf's head down into the pail of thick, dark-yellow colostrum, the calf sucking on them would begin to take in milk. Soon it was sucking eagerly, and after a day or so drank the milk on its own—no fingers in its mouth.

We did not drink or sell this extremely rich milk that the cow produced for a short time after calving, but the calf was weaned right away so that as soon as the colostrum phase was over we could give the calf a warm-water and powdered-milk mix, and the mother cow's milk could be sold.

My sister Sue took over filling the wood box, and I had a new skill and a job that I held until I went to high school. I was always glad to learn something new, and never minded this chore. It was pleasant to be in the warm barn where my father and grandfather were working, and the new calves were always lively and cute.

Later, my father transitioned to keeping registered Ayrshires, and asked me to draw the pattern of brown coloring of each new calf onto the outline of a cow to be sent off to the registration office. This was a fun job because I liked to draw, and I gave it my very best attention.

4. CONCORD

For most of my growing up our family lived on my father's family homestead in Walden which dated back five generations. It consisted of 260 acres of fields, sugarbush, woods, pasture, a couple of swamps now called *wetlands*, and apple orchards. I always felt safe and secure when I was on "our land" and slightly less so on neighboring turf.

We only moved twice in all those years — both times for economic reasons.

The first relocation was to Concord some sixty miles to the east where we spent a summer in the 40s. Apparently there was a favorable market for logs at the time, literally a "windfall" after the Great Atlantic Hurricane of 1944, and my father, grandfather, and the rest of the family picked up stakes and moved there, leaving our hired man George to milk the cows. With acres of timber lying on the ground, there was likely a Federally-financed program that made it worthwhile for loggers to harvest the timber before it rotted.

I recall my father grumbling about how much he disliked moving as he unloaded the bureaus, beds, tables, and chairs we had brought to our new house. This move in 1945 was the only time he ever had to do so except for when he moved the family from our hill farm in Walden to one in the broad, fertile Black River valley in Craftsbury in 1959. I guess he didn't have it too hard.

During our summer in Concord the menfolk were off hauling logs to the mill all day, and it fell to my mother to milk the one Jersey cow we had brought with us to provide milk for the household. There was no barn or stable with stanchions to hold the animal in place, and it was tethered to a free-standing post with a rope tied to its halter for this operation. The cow had a habit of kicking when being milked, and the chore was always taxing for my mother. After one especially trying episode she and my father must have had words about it because someone else milked that cow after that—probably my father.

It was my job to bring in the wood every night—I had to do this even here in our new place. The woodshed was quite dark, the only light being what came through the open door to the kitchen.

In the half-light I saw a cross-cut saw used for felling trees laid horizontally across something about my height. I reached up and pulled it down by one handle so it touched the ground—I guess just because I could. I left it there, and went about bringing in the wood until I tripped or stumbled against the saw, ripping a two-inch gash in my leg above the ankle. It bled profusely, and I cried—but after I said, "Now I won't have to bring in any more wood, will I?" I received little sympathy.

Even though someone else brought in the rest of the wood that night, I thought my parents were very cold-hearted. I never let on that it was me that lowered the saw to the ground, not even when my father said he was sure he had put that saw up where no one would trip over it.

I suppose I didn't speak up because I was young and was embarrassed to own up to being the cause of my injury.

The move to Craftsbury in 1959 was prompted by a requirement that farmers purchase a bulk storage tank from which the milk could be pumped directly into refrigerated trucks for transport to the creamery. While it was more efficient and less costly, i.e. more profitable for the milk handlers, this was not the case for farmers nor, according to a report by the UVM Agricultural Experiment Station, was it necessary. Because these new bulk tanks cost about $5,000, an outlay that small family farms such as ours simply could not support, a great many small holdings ceased operation at this time, including four others in our immediate neighborhood in Walden.*

Like the Nile Delta, the fields on the Black River in Craftsbury flooded every spring adding a rich layer of silt, which unlike our hill farm in Walden could support a larger herd and the now-required bulk tank.

When my parents moved to Craftsbury they chose not to sell the place in Walden, which had been in the family for over a hundred years. This was for emotional reasons on my father's part and also because there was a program whereby you could put productive farmland into something called the "Soil Bank" and be paid for allowing it to lie fallow. The aim was to reduce surpluses and stabilize farm incomes. After the Soil Bank program ended, the fields proved useful to the Craftsbury farm, for pasturing young cattle, which were loaded into a truck and transported to Walden not unlike the goats being herded to high Alpine meadows in summer in Heidi's Switzerland.

Providentially for me, their keeping the homestead enabled me stay on in Walden while I did my practice teaching in nearby Hardwick in 1959, as well as providing me with a place to live at different times in the ensuing years.

I was living there when my six siblings and I divided the farm into seven parts after my parents died, and the buildings and a few surrounding acres became my share.

*In less than 20 years the number of farms in the state declined by roughly two thirds. Counting goat and sheep dairies, there are about 600 dairy farms in Vermont today down from nearly 11,000 in the 50s.

5. ONE-ROOM SCHOOL

I attended school—all eight grades—in a white clapboard one-room schoolhouse. It faced south, and you entered through the door to the woodshed, where firewood was stacked neatly along the east and north walls.

When my grandfather Houston spoke about being set atop the stove as punishment when he misbehaved, I pictured it taking place in my schoolhouse because it had. Both he and my father had gone to this same school. Of course, it would have been in spring or fall when the stove was not lit, and it likely was a 4 or 5-foot-high Round Oak stove, a classic for many decades.

When my father spoke about having his oldest sister Leona for his teacher, again I imagined them in my school.

During my student years in the 40s a rectangular cast iron wood stove, roughly 3 feet long and 1 ½ feet wide, sat in the center of the room. A neighbor, who lived close by, came in early on winter mornings to start the fire and warm the room. Throughout the day it was up to the teacher to keep it going by stoking it with wood chunks.

A long, divided corridor—one side for girls, the other for boys—led to the outhouses in the back which were essentially wooden benches with round holes in them.

A prominent feature in the school room was a large oak cabinet mounted over the blackboard. It was always a little dramatic when the teacher unlatched the drop- down cover to reveal several rolls of wonderful, pull-down maps—The United States (48 at the time), Europe, South America, Asia, and Africa. I loved those maps with the countries, states, and provinces in bright colors. You could see where they were situated in relation to each other and get an idea of their sizes except for Greenland and Iceland, which were greatly exaggerated due to their northern location in this flattened globe.

Lillian and me 1943
(My name was Sally growing up)

The school was within walking distance for students numbering nine to twelve — at times, thirteen. We all went home for dinner — it was not called "lunch" — and had to be back at school an hour later.

One morning after an especially heavy snow overnight, my father brought around old Prince to give us a ride. The roads had not been plowed and it would have been tough walking the quarter mile to school. And so he set the three of us on Prince's bare back with bridle reins for guiding him. He told us to slide off when we got there and Prince would know to come home. Though I was skeptical, he did just that. The teacher, who was my grandmother and boarded with us, had to walk that morning in her green wool snow pants and thick one-and-a-half-inch heels and rubber overshoes that had a snap over the instep.

There were one or two pupils in each grade except for at least one grade with no one. We were there to learn reading, writing, arithmetic, spelling, and geography, but there were fun times, too. We played softball and kick-the-can in spring and fall; in winter we slid down the hill on our sleds or skis or played Fox and Geese at recess time. For this we'd make tracks in the snow in the shape of a big circle with paths into the center so that it looked like a pie. Each of us stood on the perimeter at the juncture of one of the pathways ready to dash to the nearest open spot on the ring when the fox at the center yelled "Fox and Geese!" The person who couldn't get to one that wasn't taken was now the fox.

The book wagon came every few weeks, which was a real treat. Behind the double doors at the back of the panel truck was a revolving carousel of shelves of wonderful books that none of us had seen before. We each could choose two books every time it came.

One that I remember savoring especially was *Green Mountain Boy* by Leon W. Dean. It was about Seth Warner who grew up to become a captain in the citizen militia known as the Green Mountain Boys and later a colonel in the Revolutionary War. I found his backcountry skills, honesty and bravery inspiring. He was a great hunter, had a deep knowledge of indigenous plants and herbs and, having acquired rudimentary medicinal knowledge from his doctor-father, held some sway as a healer.

Even then, I was interested in plants and herbs and transplanted wild-growing trilliums, sedum and a lady slipper to a shady spot behind our house. The lady slipper and painted trilliums, both of which are slow-growing "plants of concern" to conservationists, have disappeared, but the sedum is still there. I also made it a point to learn to identify the trees that grew on our farm, which my dad would name as we tramped through the deep snow tapping maple trees. He would size up the tree, hand drill a hole under a large overhanging branch, and drive in the spout. My job was to hang the bucket and place a cover on it.

Starting in 1949 Nabisco's shredded wheat cereal boxes contained gray cardboard dividers on which were printed "Straight Arrow's Secrets of Indian Lore and Know-How." On them were instructions and diagrams for making things like bows and arrows, starting a fire by rubbing sticks together, and tying different kinds of knots. I collected these and executed many of the plans, though I never perfected the art of starting a fire using two sticks.

My father made me a bow out of a sturdy ash branch to which he attached a rawhide bowstring. My grandmother, who became my teacher in fifth grade, gave me a jackknife with a picture of Hopalong Cassidy on the handle for Christmas one year. It had two blades and a ring through which I strung a rawhide thong that I could tether to the belt loop on my dungarees. It was a prize possession for several years. I liked to whittle, and I used it to fashion arrows out of saplings.

Shortly before Memorial Day the entire school marched to the nearby cemetery carrying new flags to place on the graves of veterans of the Revolutionary and Civil Wars. When it came my turn to carry a flag—there were only 9 veterans' graves and twelve or thirteen kids—I got to keep the one I had replaced. I found that the old flag shaft with its gold-painted topper made a superior arrow.

We would wind up the school year with a trip to Nichol's Pond for a picnic, and you could bring a fishpole. It was still too cold for swimming in early June, but it was the last day of the school year, and everyone was in a happy mood. There were sandwiches and cupcakes with frosting, and if you were lucky you might even catch a fish.

Houston Hill School photo 1946.

6. HARD TASKMASTER

It is December 1943. Teacher and eighth-grader Carrie are at the long, low table as you come into the school room from the woodshed. The rest of us, numbering twelve, are in rows on the other side of the rectangular cast iron wood stove. First-graders Angie and I are in front in the smallest desks. All of them have a ping-pong-paddle-shaped right arm rest for writing on and a shelf under the seat for books and papers. The seventh and eighth graders are in large desks in the back left corner; kids in the other grades are in medium-size desks in between.

I am three months into my first year in school, and have grown used to the low hum of the room and the occasional pop and crackle of the woodstove now that it is cold enough for a fire. I can consign to background the whispery sounds of pages being turned, the *slap* of a book being slammed closed, the exaggerated sighing and burping by the older boys, and on occasion the rattle of hail or loud splatter of raindrops against the windowpanes. And I've mostly learned to tune out the drone of someone reading aloud or giving answers to the multiplication flashcards that Teacher is holding up.

But today the hum of the room and Teacher working with Carrie at the long table is suddenly interrupted with, "OW! OW!"

It's Carrie. I look up to see Teacher pulling her hair. Yikes! Why is she doing this? I don't even know what subject they are studying, but Carrie must have given a wrong answer.

Sometimes Teacher has to say things over and over to her; it seems as though she can't seem to learn. I am shaking a little. I look at Angie, who is staring at them, wide-eyed. The room has become very still. What will happen now?

Nothing.

Teacher and Carrie go back to their lesson, and after a minute the rest of us go back to reading, doing arithmetic, or learning spelling words.

My first and second grade teacher was a hard taskmaster. She would drill us on those multiplication tables like an army sergeant. She required kids in reading class to fairly shout as they read aloud.

Was it that her style of teaching produced positive results? Or that people were impressed with her militaristic style? Perhaps it was both that led to her being named Rural School Teacher of the Year by the Vermont Association of University Women. I wonder if they would have recognized her in this way if they had known that she pulled Carrie's hair. The girl was probably at least fifteen. It never occurred to me to tell my parents about the hair-pulling.* I wish I could say I felt badly for Carrie, but I was six, and the message I got was that Teacher could be mean if you didn't do things right.

In all events, this was Carrie's last year and Teacher's next to last. I had a different teacher from third grade on.

*Since 1967 there have been no schools in Vermont with eight grades and a single teacher in one room.

7. LILLIAN

My sister Lillian died of appendicitis in 1944. She was eight, and I was seven. I was only peripherally aware of the war raging at the time. I knew about rationing and those little red or blue tokens given in change when you bought coffee or meats with stamps from a ration book. With so many items from gasoline to basic foods like sugar in limited supply due to war needs or to their sources having been cut off, rationing was a way to provide fairer distribution of what was available.

I knew that my father listened to Gabriel Heatter for war news every night on our floor-model Philco radio and that three of my uncles were in the Service; two in the Navy and one in the Army. But my dad and my uncle Jody were deferred because they were farmers and food production was also important.

I remember that we saved rags to contribute to the war effort and rag men came around occasionally to collect them. While I knew that milkweed seed pods could be sold to the government for making life preservers and vests from the floss, we never learned where to take them.*

*The fiber from kapok tree pods which had been used for flotation devices became unavailable after the East Indies was occupied by the Japanese in 1942. Now called Indonesia, these islands also had supplied the U.S. with 90 percent of its rubber up until then, causing the U.S. to quickly expand its synthetic rubber production.

I recall my sister being sick in bed—it seemed to me for days. With the shades drawn it was semi-dark and shadowy in the room. When I went in one morning she said, "Take these eggs away. They're too sweet." How could eggs be too sweet? They aren't sweet at all. I removed the eggs. We were always given a poached egg on soaked toast made with my mother's home-made bread when we were sick.

In those days our family never had store-bought sliced bread, which in any case was briefly banned in 1943 to save the one hundred tons of steel required to make slicing machines each year. However, the hue and cry over the government's attempt at this wartime conservation measure was so great that it was soon withdrawn. The major complaints were that hand-cut slices didn't fit into toasters and that serrated knives with which to cut the loaves were in short supply. According to *Time* magazine, bread-cutting instructional handouts read "like a golf lesson, 'Keep your head down. Keep your eye on the loaf. And don't bear down.'"

One day a man in a suit came to our house, and we kids were ushered into the living room with the door closed behind us. When I was a little older, I surmised he might have been the undertaker.

After he left, my father came into the living room, cleared his throat, and told us that Lillian had died. He said it quietly, simply stating the fact. He didn't say anything more. I didn't have any way to think about my sister dying. At seven, I knew what dying meant and had been upset when I first learned that I would die—that everyone has to die sometime—but I soon forgot about it. Sue, age 4, and Amy, still a baby (later we would have four more siblings) were too young to understand what was going on.

Soon I realized that when anyone mentioned Lillian's name, my mother became very quiet. I hardly ever said her name after that; I didn't want her to be sad. I puzzled how someone could be alive one minute and then just not be. But it was not the kind of thing I would talk about with my father or grandfather, and I never asked anyone

We continued to save rags for the war effort and my father continued to listen to the war news every night after chores, but everything felt different now; not warm and easy the way it had been before. No one laughed much either.

One night in mid-winter I woke with a very strong feeling that if I went down to her grave in the cemetery, I would see Lillian. I imagined slipping down the stairs and very quietly putting on my snowsuit and overshoes which were drying behind the cookstove. I did not want to wake my mother and father who slept in a bedroom off the kitchen. 1 envisioned walking the half-mile or so over the hill, past my school, and along a stretch of road that wasn't plowed in winter to the cemetery. In the end I didn't go. I knew it was a long shot that I could be quiet enough not to wake my folks, especially since I would have to leave through the kitchen door, which stuck and made a loud *ttff* sound when you opened it.

Remembering it some years later, I reflected that if I *had* managed to slip out undetected, I might have perished in the cold and snow in which case I *would* have seen my sister. In that sense perhaps my strong feeling that night wasn't wrong.

I can picture my sister's funeral—all those gladioluses with big bows that said *Niece* or *Granddaughter*, everyone around me crying, and up in front Lillian in her best dress lying in a little white bed. I have no other childhood memories of her, though she must have been around all those early years since we were only a year apart in age.

I have a few pictures of her; she had long, very light-blonde hair, and I can see that she was quite tall. I know she had blue eyes. Over the years, different aunts have told me how quick and bright Lillian was and that she, being the first grandchild, had been lavished with attention by everyone in the family. I have no recollection of any of this.

Much later, in the 1980s, I participated in a forty-day therapeutic training program called *The Ark*, in which I did a lot of therapy. One of the principal modalities employed was primal integration therapy. Remembering traumatic experiences in childhood, trainees as we were called, would re-enact them—on some level, relive them. The key difference was that in this protected space, it was safe to express feelings and talk about them in order to integrate them.

One time when I began telling my therapist for that day about my sister dying, a memory came that I'd long forgotten. Arriving home from school and not seeing my dog, I asked, "Where's Ricky?"

"He's been put to sleep," my mother said.

"Well, when will he wake up?"

"I'm afraid he won't ever wake up." She tried to comfort me, holding my face against her clean apron. She had tears in her eyes, but I was having none of it. I knew she would not have been the one responsible for Ricky being put to sleep, but as soon as I could without being rude, I fled to the haybarn, where I stared at the slices of dancing dust motes coming through the vertical boards of the walls. I stayed there for a long time not feeling anything.

It seemed that Ricky had teamed up with a neighbor's dog and killed a number of turkeys that our next-door neighbor was raising as a cash crop. My father had to pay the neighbor 50 dollars which was a lot of money at the time.

I found it hard to believe my dog would do this. I thought that if only someone had told me about it, I could have seen to it he was not out at night from then on, and he would not have had to be killed.

In relating this to my therapist on *The Ark*, I was overcome with an enormous rage. "No," I shouted. "Ricky is *my* dog! You can't do this! He's *my* dog…"

Somehow I moved on to feelings of loss and grief at losing my sister. I was engulfed in sadness. It was like being lost in a cold blue color that is everywhere and goes on forever. For the first time, I cried. After primals like this, which I sometimes repeated, I felt a quiet softness and freshness such as one experiences after a summer rainstorm. It was as though the air had cleared and there was more space.

Eventually, I came to feel love for my sister, and now when I think of her I have a hazy impression of her very light blonde hair and I see her encased in warm yellow light.

When many years later I asked my father about his having Ricky euthanized, he said that because he was a town selectman at the time, he had felt he had to. Of course, he could at least have talked to me about it. But no, I realized he really couldn't; it simply wasn't in his vocabulary of behavior to talk about something like this or even say he was sorry.

While I didn't know it at the time, Lillian's dying had also affected how I felt about my name. Over the years I had played with adopting different ones. My given name was Sally after a great aunt whom I had never met. I called myself *Ginger* when I was an adolescent and later *Diana* after the huntress in Roman mythology and because I liked the strong definite sound of the *D*. But neither one stuck.

For a while I called myself *Sarah Lovejoy,* and signed letters to friends this way. It was a family name and *love* and *joy* were words that it felt good to be associated with. I've always liked the name *Sarah* with its lift at the end — *Sar-uh,* and there was a certain logic to adopting it in that it is the proper name which gave rise to *Sally* as a shortened form. But it wasn't until I took a workshop in which we explored our relationships to our names, that I realized the reason I didn't like my birth name was because there were two *ls* in it. On a not-conscious level, I had associated Lillian's name— and, by extension, mine with its *ls*—with an uncomfortable grayness that I wanted to avoid feeling.

After the workshop I changed my name to Sarah. It was simple to do then—notify Social Security, your bank, legal, and business associations and use your new name consistently.

Sally, Susan, Amy, Lillian 1944

8. THE BAKER

When we were kids, my cousin Ruthie and I spent long hours playing and dreaming together about how we'd have a house and live together when we grew up. We said we'd have a swimming pool and swim every single day. Ruthie vowed she'd have a horse to ride, and I said I wanted to be a baker and make pies and bread and rolls.

Ruthie and I never did live together. After college she got married, and as her kids grew, opened a pre-school where she had a brook for the children to wade in, a garden, a horse, dog, ducks, chickens, and kittens.

After The University of Vermont (UVM), I went to Worcester, Massachusetts, Boston and then San Francisco to seek my fortune doing newspaper work when I could find it. My first job was in the Bay State as a "routing specialist" for an automobile club in Worcester. In San Francisco I worked in the complaint department of a large department store. After almost a year I returned East and got a job reporting for *The Worcester Telegram & Evening Gazette* and later as garden editor for *The Boston Sunday Herald*. While I was at the *Herald* the printers went on strike, effectively locking out the editorial staff. Unable to go to work, we took advantage of our "time off" and had twenty-nine parties over the thirty-one days of the strike.

At one of them I met Jack Cook, a copy editor who worked nights. But for the parties we never would have met. I was intrigued to meet someone whose parents had emigrated from England, and I suppose he was interested to meet someone with a farm background. About a year later we were married, and in due course moved to Vermont, our young son in tow.

I found work at local weeklies, and we grew a very large garden. Jack was an avid skier and hiker, and while living in Boston we spent many exuberant weekends in New Hampshire and Vermont enjoying these sports. But after we moved north and Jack began freelance writing for various magazines, there rarely seemed to be time or money for them.

Neither Ruthie nor I ever had that elusive swimming pool. She did have a horse for many years, and I spent a few summers early on with my sister Sue and family at their farm on Nantucket where one year I worked as a baker. At Provisions Bakery I made French bread, croissants and muffins every single day. I would saunter across the parking lot to the A&P to pick up fresh fruits for my muffin creations—Peach-Nutmeg, Cranberry-Lime, Zucchini-Orange Zest, and Ginger-Peach—along with the standards: Blueberry, Raisin Bran, and Apple Walnut.

One day a tradesman leaned in at the kitchen door to tell me my muffins were the "best on the island." Later that summer a yachtsman told me my French bread was the "best on the East Coast." Gratifying to say the least, and I too, had fulfilled one of my childhood dreams.

I loved the autonomy and creativity the job afforded and basked in the compliments, but it was a one-off; I had long since set my sights on a writing life.

Though our lives spun out in different directions, my cousin Ruthie and I remained good friends until she died a few years ago.

9. HIGH SCHOOL

We lived five miles from Hardwick Academy where I attended high school. For my first three years, I lived with a family near Hardwick where I worked for my board. My mother had done this, and I surmise that my parents thought this was just what you do if you live out of town. I can find no other reason since I could have ridden with my neighbor and classmate Gerry, whose father drove him to school until he got his license and could drive himself.

While working for my board solved the transportation issue, I was not always happy about it. First, it meant I couldn't play basketball, which I desperately wanted to do.

Second, I would come home from school every day and immediately have to wash all day's dishes, as well as clean up after supper. But the worst part was that on Saturday mornings I had to vacuum the entire house. I still abhor vacuuming and do an absolute minimum of it. It's the noise, the dry air, and the boring drudgery I associate with what felt like hours of vacuuming every single Saturday.

Third, I think that for Phyllis, the mother of two kids in the two-parent home where I boarded, it was a transaction. I suppose it was, but I often felt lonely in that house. Phyllis was nice, but didn't care to talk to me beyond instructing me regarding what she wanted done.

One day I came home and began to tell her how we had elected officers in my class. I could see she didn't understand why I was going on about this, and after that I didn't try to tell her anything. By noon on Saturdays, with the vacuuming done, I could go home where my mother was interested to hear everything I wanted to tell her.

It wasn't until my senior year that I was able to live at home and play basketball. Though I was tall and was a fairly good player, I hadn't played those previous three years when I might have developed some skill. Although I was on the team, was able to practice, and wore a shiny gold and purple uniform at games, I got to play in very few of them.

10. HAYING TIME

It is August 1955. The team of horses draws the wagonload of hay into the haybarn, hooves thudding hollowly on the thick plank floor over the stable.

"Whoa," my dad says, when the load of loose hay is squarely underneath the start of the metal track that runs along the underside of the barn ridgepole. The horses know to stand patiently while the loose hay is unloaded. The fragrant smell of new hay is all around me as I get up from my soft nest atop the load. Riding in from the field high up on the swaying, lurching hay wagon with the harness tug chains jangling on the down-grades is utter bliss.

My father and the hired man, pitchforks in hand, head to the back of the barn where they will distribute the hay in the bays on either side. My mother, watching for us out the kitchen window, has brought our third workhorse, Babe, around for unloading.

I am a little keyed up because I have a date tonight to see a movie with my third cousin Sonny, who is home on leave from the Army. But there is plenty of time, I remind myself. This is the last load of the day, and he won't be coming until 6:30. I don't know him well, but he's a known quantity because he's a relative, and I had seen him at family reunions when I was younger.

I get to work hauling the jangly hayfork down to the load of hay from the track which runs along the roof line. It is my job to set the large steel hay fork in an X-shape into the load of hay. I slide each of the four curved tines deep into the hay and then jump on it so it has a good sturdy grip. If it is not done right, the forks can let go of the hay bundle on its way up to the track, and I'll have to set them all over again.

"All set," I signal to my mother outside, as I step back from the fork. She has driven Babe into position facing away from the big open door and the load of hay. Having hooked the whiffletree onto the thick rope-and-pulley arrangement emanating from the right side of the barn, she drives Babe some fifty feet, the horse straining mightily as the heavy forkful of hay rises. Once it reaches the track it zings along merrily to where the men are, and my father calls, "Trip it."

I give the light trip-rope a firm yank, which pulls the little chain connecting the tines, and releases them. The hay falls with a big *whump* raising a cloud of chaff and hay dust where the men are waiting.

"Whoa," my mother says to Babe. She unhooks the whiffletree so the rope can return through the pulleys as I haul the clanging empty fork back down to the load for the operation to be repeated.

I watch the last forkful go up without a hitch. But time has been passing, and Sonny has appeared, all spiffed up in his tan Army clothes. He stands grinning as, embarrassed, I climb down from the wagon all sweaty and grimy. I'm in my jeans and work shirt, my hair uncombed.

"I'll just be a couple minutes," I tell him as I fly to the house to wash my face, change into a skirt and blouse, comb my hair, and put on lipstick.

I don't remember what movie we saw, and I didn't go out with him again although I would have if my mother hadn't told my father what I had told her—that Sonny wanted to park and make out after the show, and I had refused. My mother relayed to me that my dad thought it best I didn't make any more dates with him.

I had not been out on casual dates like this very much. I was very shy, and tended to freeze up and become tongue-tied around boys. Sonny wasn't bad-looking, but I had no special interest in him, and when he called again, I didn't feel badly telling him I couldn't go out with him.

Of course, I didn't think about it then, but I realize now that with their oldest daughter being in this new dating phase, my young parents were probably finding their way.

Sally, Susan, Amy, Judy, Gary, Anne, Rebecca

11. WHERE THERE'S A WILL . . .

I was a second child for my first seven years. As such I was not groomed to be first—first in our family to go to high school, then to college, and finally to leave home and get a job. Paving the way after my sister Lillian died was not without stress. The day I began high school I missed two classes. I had come from a rural one-room school with eight grades totaling twelve or thirteen kids, and suddenly I was a freshman in a class of thirty-eight in a system where you changed rooms for every subject. Confusing at first, but I soon learned the ropes.

My father, who rarely attended any of my school functions after I left elementary school, came to my high school graduation. While I did not take top honors, I did receive a special commendation for being a good student, exemplifying character, diligence, and good citizenship. As he went through the line, shaking hands and congratulating the graduates, he told me, "Your mother and I are proud of you." I beamed. I glowed. It was a high point of my graduation from high school, the more so perhaps because of an incident one summer during those high school years.

I was raking the scatterings in order to salvage what was left after the wagon and hay-loader had been through. I was raking with the one-horse dump rake, and though I knew you were supposed to rake against the direction the mowing machine cutter-bar had taken on its first course around the field, I somehow had gotten confused and was raking the wrong way.

"If you keep on going to school, pretty soon you won't know anything at all," my dad said. It hurt.

In later years I learned that he and his brother Jody had not been given the opportunity to attend high school after graduating from eighth grade the way his sisters had. Perhaps this explained his attitude. His father had said he needed the boys to help him on the farm. I suppose he expected them to be farmers and thought they would have no need for further schooling. His oldest sister, Leona, who had taught my dad in grammar school, said he was very bright and really should have gone to high school and beyond.

During my freshman year at UVM, I found that when I went home for breaks, I would fall into a funk after I returned. The contrast between our lives at home and my pursuits in college was profound. I felt down—almost depressed. I think it was some combination of feeling I was betraying my family by participating in this activity so foreign to our way of life and guilt that I was part of an enterprise that stood in such stark contrast to my humble origins. I have since read that this kind of thing may happen when the student is from a family where no one had previously attended college.

I found it hard to understand my high school friend Bonnie's choosing to leave UVM after only one semester. Her family had supported her going there 100 per cent, whereas it had been a struggle for me to attend. I could have gone to Lyndon State Teachers' College, as it was called then, with my parents' blessing; tuition was affordable and the school was not far away. My father said, "Your mother and I think you ought to be a nurse or a teacher since both your grandmothers were teachers and your Aunt Olive is a nurse."

Trouble was, I didn't want to be a nurse *or* a teacher, and I did want to take courses in Latin and Greek, neither of which was offered at Lyndon. I had loved my high school

Latin courses; unlike English with all its vagaries and exceptions, it was possible to learn just about everything about the language. And because Latin and Greek were foundational to so many English words, I thought they would be useful in writing.

However, with the help and encouragement of my favorite teacher, Mrs. Cobb, who taught Latin, French, and English, I applied for and received a scholarship through the Wilbur Fund. With this $400 per semester, together with enrolling in education (lower tuition), and securing housing in the only co-op dorm on campus (students rotated cooking lunch and dinner in return for discounted food and housing fees), I was able to attend the school of my choice, UVM, and take the courses I wanted.

My parents' income was $5,000 per year in 1955. Even allowing for cost-of-living differences and that the farm provided our milk and beef, I knew it was low given there were ten of us including my grandfather. I was given bus money to come home for holidays and breaks, but I really could not expect more.

Over the next eleven years my mother drove one or another of us to our state university together with the basics: bedding, desk lamp, snack food and a little metal coil with a cord you could plug into an outlet for making a hot drink. By the time my youngest sibling, Becky finished, five of us had graduated from UVM. My sister Amy trained as a nursing assistant and later went back to school to become a registered nurse. Gary, the boy in the family, graduated from Vermont Technical College.

He had been seriously injured in a Volkswagen rollover with some of his high school friends his senior year in high school. Fortunately, he recovered well, but the thinking at the time was that he should have training for non-physical work in the event he would be unable to do farm work. After graduating, he joined my father running the farm in

Craftsbury, and eventually he took it over. Meanwhile the Viet Nam War was raging. Farmers were no longer exempt from Military Service, but because there was a draft lottery at the time and Gary's birth year was not chosen, he did not serve in the Viet Nam War.

After my struggle to go to a college of my choice, it was accepted that the rest would do so to the extent it was possible. My mother, especially, recognized that each of us was different and supported our desires accordingly.

12. CROSSING THE ALPS WITH HANNIBAL

It was quite late at night when we arrived at the Swiss-Italian border. There were three of us sisters—Sue, myself, and Judy, who was taking a semester off from attending UVM in order to make the trip to Europe with us. Sue had been working at a US Army Special Services post in France and had purchased the Volkswagen bug in which we were traveling. I had evolved a pattern of working at various jobs just long enough to save for a trip, and since I often worked only part of a year I usually got a tax refund, which also supported my travels. Securing a new job when I returned was not difficult in the 60s.

Having left behind numerous charming old-world villages in the Swiss Alps and zipped through remote valley hamlets, we began ascending high mountain passes. We marveled at how Hannibal could have maneuvered thirty-seven elephants through them. According to the Greek historian Polybius, the famed General also marched some 30,000 troops, 9,000 horses and the many pack animals needed to supply such an expedition through these Alpine passages. *

Crossing the Rhone was no mean feat either considering the number of foot soldiers that had to be ferried over in small boats plus cavalry in their larger craft with horses

*More than twenty centuries on historians are still marveling over Hannibal's boldness   (See footnote next page)

swimming behind. And then there were all those elephants that had to be floated across on rafts.

Crossing these same Alps in 1964 (though not in Hannibal's footsteps) my sisters and I found the views breathtaking — and frightening. The guardrails along the narrow roads looked flimsy as we peered down thousand-foot vertical cliffs at tiny Alpine lakes below — outlooks that would give a mountain goat vertigo.

We were headed for a small *pensione* (bed and breakfast) in a town over the border in Italy, which we had gleaned from our trusty guidebook *Europe on Five Dollars a Day* (ha, I say as I write this in 2025). But as the day faded to evening and then dark of night, we began to wonder if we would ever reach our destination.

Sue and I were in the front seat when we were stopped by two men in dark green uniforms, who shone their blinding-bright flashlights in our eyes and indicated we should open

---

and ingenuity in trekking those elephants north from what is now eastern Spain, across the Rhone River into Gaul (now France), and on through the Alps into Italia. The much shorter route to Rome by boat was not feasible given that the Carthaginians did not have enough vessels and the Romans controlled all the ports on the Mediterranean.

While the route he took through the Alps in 218 BCE has been disputed for centuries, with the discovery in 2016 of a "mass animal deposition" occurring within the time-frame of Hannibal's crossing, researchers now believe his path was through the Col de Traversette.

As Hannibal descended into hostile Roman territory on the Italian peninsula, inflicting "shock and awe" with his enormous beasts, he scored some stunning victories. Nevertheless, having suffered significant losses in the Alpine crossing and unable to muster reinforcements for his army due to Rome controlling the ports, he ultimately succumbed to the prowess of the Romans.

the door to the back seat. I don't know what they were expecting, but what they found was Judy, tousled and bug-eyed from being roused from sleep in the middle of the night. We didn't know why they had stopped us or what they wanted, but it soon became clear that they didn't speak any English. While we had all had high-school French, Sue, a smattering of Spanish, and I knew Latin and a little Greek, none of us knew Italian.

After brief exchanges beginning with their speaking in rapid Italian, followed by our *Je ne comprends pas* we soon arrived at a stalemate with one of the men yelling, "*Douane! Douane!*" as he fixed me with his dark Gallic eyes. I didn't know any word resembling *douane*, but he kept repeating it, and somewhere in the murky flotsam of foreign cultures and languages swimming around in my brain, spurred by the intensity with which he enunciated the word over and over, a spark was struck. "Border!" I blurted out. His face relaxed. He smiled and, accompanied by more rapid-fire Italian, proceeded to show us on our map how we needed to turn on to a different route which would bring us to a proper crossing.

We were only too happy to follow orders. Our adrenaline still running high as we drove more miles, we conjectured that the reason we couldn't continue on our original route might have been that it was closed for the winter. We *were* in the Alps, after all. In due course we passed into Italy at the designated point without incident, found our *pensione*, and crawled gratefully into lofty feather beds. Heavenly!

I have found out since that *douane* is French for customs, not a word I had encountered in my year of high school French. When he heard me say border, perhaps he heard *bordo*, Italian for margin or edge. In any case, the word *douane* is etched firmly in my mind these sixty years on.

13. THREE FLIGHTS UP

When our son was born, Jack and I were living in a fourth-floor walk-up apartment on Henchman Street in Boston's North End. It was an Italian neighborhood with lots of colorful little stores—butcher shops, bread shops, bars and restaurants, a barbershop, a dry goods store, and a laundromat. All were within easy walking distance of our flat. Being on the top floor we had easy access to the roof where we liked to entertain on warm summer evenings.

On feast days a beautiful child-like, larger-than-life statue of the saint being celebrated would be paraded through the streets to the beat of a makeshift band as people attached dollar bills to her clothing.

I didn't mind the stairs, and our apartment was nice and light, but I did feel for the diaper service delivery guy, who I expect dreaded the weekly three-flight walkup. At least he could carry the really heavy bag *down* those flights.

My sister Judy, who lived across town, was dating a Black man at the time, and I invited the two of them to dinner one night. The next morning all four tires on our Volkswagen were slashed and the windshield was shattered. We had no proof, but believed that someone in the neighborhood did not like Black people coming into their territory, and this was their way of showing it. Our insurance company said they would pay this time but would not cover any such destruction in the future.

After climbing those stairs every day for the nine months prior to the birth, all the while incrementally adding weight, my leg muscles were so finely tuned that I was able to bound up those stairs like a gazelle in the first weeks after the baby was born.

I recall one time in those new-mother days being out doing errands by myself with Jack minding the babe at home. As I wended my way along the narrow streets of the North End, busily checking off items on my list, I remembered with a start that I had a baby at home! How could I have forgotten, even for an instant? The wonder of it.

Baby Jere learned to negotiate those stairs at an early age. I would put him in his stroller and do my laundry and shopping, but when I came home it was a challenge to bring him and everything else up the three flights in one trip. The alternative was to put him in his crib and make a second trip. The vestibule at the bottom was tiny and opened right onto the street—not safe to leave items there for long. Once Jeremiah was able to creep pretty well, I would set him on the bottom stair, me right behind him with my bundles and bags, and together we would slowly make our way up to the third floor. He loved doing this, and it solved the problem.

Jeremiah

14. IS THE REVOLUTION TONIGHT?

Early in the heady days of the Women's Liberation Movement in Boston — Jack and I still in the North End and Jeremiah a toddler — I joined a women's consciousness-raising group. After our first few gatherings I remember being in a blind rage for about a week, realizing how women in general have been held down and how I in particular had been affected by a systemic patriarchal culture. Jack was generally in accord with the aims of the Movement, but evinced resistance to making changes on the home front beyond occasionally making a dish for supper.

One evening as I prepared to leave for my women's group meeting, Jack took phone calls one after another — all of them for me. "Is the Revolution *tonight*?" he asked, handing me the phone for the fourth time.

In due course, I attended a colloquium on the major issues of the day, organized by Bread and Roses Collective in Cambridge.

Picture a huge auditorium filled to capacity with women waiting for the program to commence when an announcement comes from the podium that there is a man in the room followed by a request that he leave — immediately. Everyone cranes her neck looking to see who the interloper is. I hadn't been aware of a male presence among us, but soon spotted him. Nothing belligerent or hostile-appearing about him — a blonde fellow of medium height and build probably in his 40s. I'm guessing he thought the event warranted being described to a wider audience and that he was the one to do it. In any case, when he demurred at being asked to leave, he was promptly and unceremoniously hustled from the room, a husky, no-nonsense woman on either side of him.

I had not seen women asserting themselves in quite this way before and found it breathtaking and exhilarating. At the same time I felt a twinge of compassion for the guy. It can't have been fun to be physically dispatched from the room before several hundred women.

15. THE COMMUNE YEARS

On any given day in 1970 in a three-story house on the Roxbury-Boston line, you might find someone in the kitchen making dinner and someone in the living room playing with the children—there were five under the age of six, including a newborn. The other seven adults were either working or attending meetings. On the wall in the kitchen was a work wheel, which laid out who had which chore that day, including housekeeping. This communal group was the second of three cooperative living arrangements that Jack and I were part of in the early '70s.

Beyond the front door of our house the world was on fire with political activity of every stripe—women's lib consciousness-raising groups, Black Panthers, Students for a Democratic Society (SDS), and Bread and Roses to name a few. Also, there was a ferment of experimentation with alternative lifestyle practices—open marriages, serial monogamy, multi-level relationships, cooperative pre-schools, kibbutz-style compounds, organic food purists, vegetarians, vegans, and yoga classes, to name a few. And let's not forget the rallies, teach-ins and marches for and against segregation in the schools and to protest the country's involvement in the Vietnam War.

The idea for sharing living space with others took root in a series of meetings that Jack and I had attended with four other couples. The women, steeped in Women's Liberation concepts of sharing domestic work and childrearing equally with their spouses, were looking for a model beyond the nuclear family that would better support this goal.

The men in the group—a psychologist, an urban planner, a free-lance writer, and a human services worker (one couple had dropped out)—were at least nominally committed to the idea. The driving force behind the venture were the women, who included an artist and stay-at-home mom with the newborn, a member of the women's health collective that had published *Our Bodies Ourselves*, a member of a political action committee, a grad student, and myself— ever in search of free-lance writing projects after the *Boston Herald* downsized and I was laid off.

Cooperative living schemes were part of the zeitgeist of the times, although most were in country settings and had a strong back-to-the-land component. Jack and I had met with the other couples over the winter to discuss purchasing a house together for living communally. As spring approached we found one in Roxbury that was feasible cost-wise. But buying it was going to take some time, and when Jack heard about a summer commune forming on Massachusetts' South Shore we decided to check it out.

This ad hoc living arrangement had begun with a few core households getting together to rent a down-at-the-heels hotel for the summer on the beach in Manomet. Basically if someone in the group vouched for you and you paid the rent for a bedroom, you could have it for the season. We signed on.

Except for the dry, crumbling swimming pool and constant plumbing issues, the place was fine; the rambling old building was clean, and the roof didn't leak. The number of residents fluctuated between twelve and twenty-five men, women, and children ages two to sixty-five. People came and went; some stayed a few days or a couple of weeks, others like us were there for the summer. Always the number soared on weekends. You paid by the day, week, or summer. We rented two rooms because Jack needed an office for his free-lance writing business.

We slept on mattresses on the floor. At first we had Jeremiah sleeping on a mat in our room, but it soon became clear that there was no putting him to bed at a reasonable hour and expecting him to stay there. There was a bedroom designated for all the children that contained a built-in bed, fashioned from odds and ends of lumber about three feet off the floor. This make-shift crib left by some earlier tenant of the hotel worked much better.

The people in the group were a colorful mix that included several families and single people from Cambridge who were involved in the Women's Movement or in Vietnam War protests. Among them were a college teacher and his homemaker wife and two kids. She told me that she and her husband were both comfortable with an arrangement whereby he spent regular time with a single woman-friend whereas she had no interest in pursuing a relationship outside their marriage. There was also a single mom with boys ages eight and ten, a classical music radio host who came every weekend with a lady on his arm, and various other single men and women, some with children.

One of the people that stayed for a while was a guy we called Chuck, a tall, serious, rather handsome man. He did not use his real name, we were told, because he was a member of the Weathermen, a far-left faction of SDS, and was on an FBI wanted-list. This lent him a certain mystique.

A great many tortillas were made that summer on the gigantic cast-iron range in the kitchen. There was lots of music, weed, women's-lib talk, and experimenting with all manner of relationships within and outside marriage. Jack and I were not interested in exploring multilateral relationships, but I was fascinated to hear about what others were doing. The women I spoke with all seemed to be comfortable with any arrangement they were part of.

When a young couple, who had backpacked across the country with their baby, hitchhiking and foraging for food the entire way (their bible was a thick book on wild edible plants), heard about our summer commune, they joined us for a few weeks. I noted that the apple-cheeked child, who was about a year old and nursing, was all muscle and bone—not an iota of fat anywhere. He was bright-eyed, remarkably strong and agile and showed no ill effects whatsoever from his nomadic lifestyle.

A young grad student shared that she was struggling with a question her professor had posed when she departed for the summer, "When are you going to take charge of your own life?" It was a question I asked myself from time to time after that. Some years later it came to me that I was doing what I had always wanted to do; I had a nice garden and was actively engaged in writing. Indeed, I had taken charge of my life.

Toward the end of the summer one of the couples decided to take LSD; a first time for both of them. A number of us were present, and it was fascinating to witness the effect the drug had on the two of them as they progressed from overwhelming wonder and awe at the amazing colors they were seeing, to seemingly unstoppable hilarity, to fear and paranoia when it was rumored that the cops might be coming. The police never did arrive, but it put a damper on the event and everyone soon dispersed.

I concluded that if one is going to take LSD, it is very important that it be done in a safe, protected place, because the least whiff of danger could turn the experience from euphoria to a bad trip.

That autumn Jack and I and Jeremiah moved from this summer commune in Manomet into our newly purchased three-decker in Roxbury's Mission Hill district together with seven other adults and four children. It was located in what was called a "changing neighborhood" meaning it was moving from an all-white, largely Irish area to a mixed Black and White one. For our group it simply meant we could afford to buy a house there; we were not concerned about who might be living next door.

This was a far more structured communal household than the one in Manomet, and we presumed that it would go on forever. That assumption, I believe, was our first mistake. There is something about not having an escape route laid out that exacerbates the pressure cooker effect of living with unrelated adults, even ones that have come together with agreed-upon ideals and reasons.

While the allure of living communally had stemmed from the idea that doing so would provide for couples sharing domestic chores and childrearing equally, economic savings were also a factor. Having one washing machine, stove, refrigerator, etc., for some fourteen people and dividing heating bills and mortgage payments four ways were also selling points. But these did not come close to outweighing the nuclear-family conditioning that all of us had grown up with, not to mention our cultural differences, disparate backgrounds, and personalities.

Household work was shared quite equably, though the work wheel had to be altered at times to accommodate people's job schedules and meetings. Being as self-reliant as possible was one of the guiding philosophies of the group and of that period. But Irv, a psychologist, declared he had zero interest in learning to do plumbing and would pay out of pocket to avoid it. We had many house meetings about how to handle this and other issues. The men, including Jack, participated in the work wheel. Irv, however, never did wield a pipe wrench during that time.

As the weeks and months rolled on, two of the couples decided to explore multilateral relationships—not with others in the group, but with people outside it. It soon appeared that we straight ones were the "neatniks" compared with the open-marriage experimenters, who were more casual about housekeeping. While the extra-marital liaisons were not an issue (I was never even aware of them), housekeeping and children's behavior were often points of contention. One of the 2-year-olds took to biting when he was fighting with another child, setting off emotional exchanges among the parents. After nine months in which we struggled valiantly and held countless "house meetings" (as though we could talk ourselves beyond generations of conditioning as nuclear families), come spring we had all pretty much had it.

Irv and Paula and their two children found single-family housing in Boston. Roland and Mary moved into an apartment and continued to do activist work. Jack and I and Bob and Karen, bitten by the back-to-the-land bug, began to search for a place where we could continue to live communally and also grow our own food.

Our search for a small place in the country on which we could realize our dream of living on the land took us far and wide. We visited countless prospective farms in northern New England and New York, gleaned from listings of rural properties in *Uncle Henry's*, a small publication found in grocery and convenience stores. This was after first looking around in Vermont where we found that farm prices were beyond our reach.

We traveled to Upstate New York to look at a 100-acre farm priced at $5,000. A bargain in many ways, it was mostly open fields in good tilth and boasted corn cribs and grain storage structures. It had its drawbacks though; in the first place none of us aspired to raising crops as serious farmers, secondly the first floor of the house had been gutted and was chock-full of tractors, a combine, harrows, plows, and sundry other farm equipment. We would need to build a house in order to live there. But it was the location that nixed the deal for me. Northern New York was about a six-hour drive from my family's location in Vermont and ten hours from Boston. I couldn't imagine living so far from the coast. I felt lonely and claustrophobic just thinking about it.

Another place we looked at was in far northern Maine. This, too was advertised in *Uncle Henry's*, the go-to publication for back-to-the-landers looking for real estate. We stayed overnight with a young couple and their two-year-old, who were living near the land we had come to see. It was boggy although there were dry areas suitable for siting a house. But listening to mosquitos the size of bumblebees divebomb my bedroom window screen all night long made me certain this was not a viable place for us. Gardening figured heavily in our homesteading plans, and I could see that bee helmet and gloves notwithstanding, much of the time it would be hell working outside.

In the end we were joined by a third couple that Jack and I knew from our Boston days, and we bought an inexpensive farm in West Peru, Maine.

It was a rather forlorn old farmhouse on twenty-five acres of cut-over hardwoods. It was located near Rumford, and we soon discovered that when the wind was right, our place smelled like that papermill town.

That, however, was the least of it. It was a cold house. On really frigid days there was frost on the inside wall of the dining nook. I had bought Dr. Denton footed pajamas for Jeremiah, but after I discovered his vaporizer making snow on his outer blanket one bitter morning, we moved him into our room.

Since he and Robbie were both two years old and about the same size, we put their clothes into one bureau—one drawer for socks, another for trousers, and so on.

"Look Mama, twins!" Jeremiah crowed as I helped him put on two socks that happened to match. Another time as we portioned out tasks for the day—designating who would make lunch or dinner, stack wood, work on winterizing the drafty house with plastic sheeting, clean the chimney, etc., Robbie, alert to everything that was going on, piped up, "You work; we play."

"That's right, Robbie," his dad affirmed.

Bob was keen to get one of the de-commissioned U.S. mail trucks that were available at discounted prices, and the purchase proved useful for transporting firewood. We hauled countless loads of hardwood rejects from a local bobbin mill to burn in our wood stoves. We bought a fifty-pound bag of lentils, and to this day I don't care if I never eat another one of those healthy legumes.

Frustrated in my attempts to write fiction, I turned to what I understood as *automatic writing* according to W.B. Yeats' and his wife Georgiana's experience with it. It didn't help my attempts at writing fiction, but I liked doing it and included some of the little poems that emanated from it in a poetry booklet that I put together later.

One day, unannounced, Bob's nephew Billy came sauntering up our road. He was just sixteen and one cool dude in his broad-brimmed leather hat and vest. Soon joined by his passionate, piano-playing buddy, Glenway, they cleaned out and moved into what had been a chicken house at the farm. Not long afterward, having located a piano in a second-hand shop in town, they told how they had gotten silver dollars at the bank and had counted out 50 of them one-by-one in payment. They brought it home on the back of their old flatbed truck *Eli*, Glenway playing that piano the entire way. They were fun and funny and lightened the mood for a while, but after several weeks they loaded up their piano and headed for Colorado.

There was a period when Jack was the object of a lot of criticism in meetings. It was very painful for him. I don't recall the reasons, but in hindsight believe it was simply that amid the myriad frustrations of trying to live communally, he became a scapegoat, albeit unconsciously. I supported

Jack unreservedly until over time the situation resolved. I realized that when the chips are down, the couple unit superseded any loyalty to the group.

There were conflicts between the other two couples, and over time it became clear that being "neat" and monogamous and having one washing machine to serve three families was not going to be enough to hold this group together, either. By spring, Ted and Carol had moved back to Newburyport, and Bob and Karen were making plans to move to West Virginia, nearer to her home state of Kentucky. We parted ways and sold the farm, and Jack and I and Jeremiah decamped to Vermont where we addressed ourselves to homesteading in Walden on the farm where I had grown up.

I had learned that it is exceedingly difficult to live communally especially if you try to do this when you already have a family. If I were to try it again I would build in an escape route; i.e. commit to a year or some finite trial period after which I could leave gracefully if I so chose.

During those commune years none of us had had any training or understanding of group process, and we were unable to stand apart from the immersive experience and see what was going on with any clarity.

Looking back I think the best thing for me about living with others was how vital and alive I felt. I experienced myself vibrantly and three-dimensionally in my daily interactions with the other adults and children; notably different from relating to one adult and child and being alone and in my head a lot of the time. I realize now that the lack of stimulation living in a single-family household in a rural setting is something that should be addressed head-on.

Though it seems much longer, in all we spent a scant two years living with other families. Some of us stayed in touch for a while afterward. Irv and Paula and family visited us in

Vermont a few times, and Jack and I and Jeremiah made a trip to West Virginia to visit Bob and Karen and their kids, but gradually distance and the new patterns of our lives took over, and we lost touch.

My take all these years later is that we were too old, too married, and perhaps too straight with regard to drugs. I think that people who were single, younger, and a part of the drug culture, or who had a core spiritual ideal or mission, tended to fare better — at least their communal households lasted longer. I think that having separate dwellings on communally owned land also helped some of them.

But a shiny dream with all the efficiencies it promises, dies hard. Jack and I continued to read about rural communes seeking people to join them (I more than he), but we did not rush in a fourth time. As the months stretched into years we found satisfaction in growing a large garden, keeping bees, sugaring, and living on the land as a plain old nuclear family. Jack continued to freelance; I found work reporting for *The Hardwick Gazette*. In this next phase we helped organize a food coop, a cooperative preschool, a farmers' market, and generally joined with others to create community.

16. COMING HOME

The first time I left home was to attend UVM in Burlington in 1955. Soon after that I went to Springfield, Massachusetts and later to Boston to find work. I have left home and come back more than a dozen times over the decades.

One of these was when Jack and I and Jeremiah, age five, moved from Boston to my family homestead in Vermont in 1973. In the early days after we arrived I would often replay a childhood scene in which I would come in from doing my chores in the barn in the evening and stop to drink in the loveliness of the hollyhocks all blossomed out in rose pinks and creams and burgundy. They were flowers I had planted along the east end of the house.

I was amazed to find them—or an iteration of them—still growing some twenty years on. They had crossed and recrossed so many times that they were virtually black. I had also transplanted sedum, trilliums, and Dutchman's breeches from the wild to a shady spot behind the house. It pleased me to find the sedum still growing there, as well.

I found work as a stringer for various newspapers, including the *Chronicle* in Barton for which I was tasked with covering a hearing regarding the Act 250 land-use law. The opening of I-89 and I-91 had made access to the state much easier and had raised concerns that it would result in profuse and chaotic development, which in fact, was already occurring in southern Vermont. The law was passed in 1970 to regulate the transfer of real estate, but controversy raged on and informational hearings were being held around the state.

At the hearing in the 70s my father sat beside me as I took notes for an article I'd be writing for *The Chronicle*. I was acutely aware that he was proud of me in my role as reporter covering the proceedings, and that while his views allowed for putting the brakes on rampant development by out-of-state interests, his sympathies lay with the other farmers whose land by and large constituted their savings. Now that there was a market for real estate, they felt they should be able to cash in without impediment. I understood the viewpoint completely.

At the same time I subscribed to the view of the proponents of the Act, who sought among other things to preserve the rural nature of the state with its patchwork of forests and green fields, by setting guidelines pertaining to how land could be bought and sold.

In this conflict and many other less significant ones I found myself agreeing with newcomers while understanding the native Vermonters' points of view. As a reporter, however, I knew to set my opinions aside and stick to the facts as I saw them.

In those days most towns still elected officers and voted budgets from the floor, and I witnessed some very heated exchanges at town meetings. At times I felt as though I was the only one with a foot on both sides of the divide.

It felt lonely.

17. RIGHT DOWN TO SUMMER

In this scene Jeremiah is four or five — that liminal stage when children still have one foot in the dreamworld of childhood.

My dad has brought his tractor from Craftsbury (he had moved the family there in 1959) and is sugaring with Jack and me, who are living at the family homestead in Walden. They are out gathering sap in a 4-by-5-by-3-foot-high metal gathering tank mounted on a hand-made platform on the back of the tractor.

Jere and I are in the kitchen. It is obvious the men are having trouble because we can hear the tractor motor grinding as the large, rubber-tired wheels spin in the deep snow. Jere is standing on a chair in front of the sink window in order to get a grandstand view of the operation.

"Mom, look," he says excitedly, not taking his eyes off the scene. "They went right down to summer!"

Sure enough, a large swath of black soil is clearly visible against the snow-covered field. In struggling to get up the rise, the tractor has churned away the snow and gone "right down to summer."

Another time he asked me out of the blue, "What is the last number?" Before I could think how to respond, he said, "Oh, I know — it's when you die."

I didn't have a better answer.

18. GROWING PEAS FOR MARKET

The fields on my family homestead in Walden have weathered many vicissitudes. After being cleared of trees for subsistence farming in the 1700s, pastured for sheep in the 1800s, and cultivated for growing hay this past century, in 1973 Jack and I decided to grow a quarter acre of peas for the farmers' market in Hardwick. In order to produce them at this scale we had to cultivate new ground, and without thinking beyond finding a nice level space, chose a spot in the center of the field behind our house. Not a good move.

As my dad and brother Gary gravely surveyed the newly planted ground spang in the middle of a field they didn't say much, but it was apparent they were not pleased. They hayed this meadow along with others each summer and trucked the crop to Craftsbury for livestock feed. Not only did they lose the hay they would have harvested on this plot, but its location made it awkward to operate haymaking machinery around it.

"Presumptuous," Jack termed it. Presumptuous on our part to cultivate that section without consulting them beforehand.

We did get a fine crop of peas, though we didn't exactly make a killing selling them. I found that picking peas at market scale is arduous, tiresome work and was not something I was eager to repeat. I called it "lessons learned." We allowed the pea plot to return to hay the following year, and we were all happier for it.

Mom and Dad

One positive part of the experiment was that I had marked off a little corner section of the plot so that Jeremiah, age 5, could plant a few beans, lettuces and radishes. He was into it. I had heard that the vibe that young children bring to growing things translates into the plants doing surprisingly well. I had to agree; his little garden proved to be amazingly lush and healthy.

Sometime after the 60s when the fields were put into the Soil Bank program, the two little fields around my house were rented to a man in town for horse pasture. I liked having the horses around. I'd look up from gardening or see them out the window munching grass and hanging out companionably. Sometimes the bay would rest her head across the black's neck. Endearing.

As the summer wore on and they ate the grass closer and closer to the ground, they began to reach under the fence surrounding my vegetable garden, and a couple of times they got into it. The damage was mostly from stomping on plants with their big hooves. Distressing nonetheless.

My father told the renter to reinforce the fence to keep the horses out, and he promptly complied. No more horses in the garden after that.

Late in the summer the man sold one of the horses and a week later   brought in a new one. Round and round the fields the two of them thundered for what seemed like hours. I had never seen horses act this way. I wondered if they were experiencing a confluence of surprise, fear, and the strangeness of being with a new horse—or perhaps joy. Maybe their feelings were just too intense to contain, and they were doing the only thing they could to alleviate the tension—run it off.

I have since learned that if unacquainted horses are brought together abruptly without a barrier between them—as these were—at first they will race or sometimes battle as a way of establishing pecking order. I'm glad these two did not fight. The next day they were munching grass together companionably.

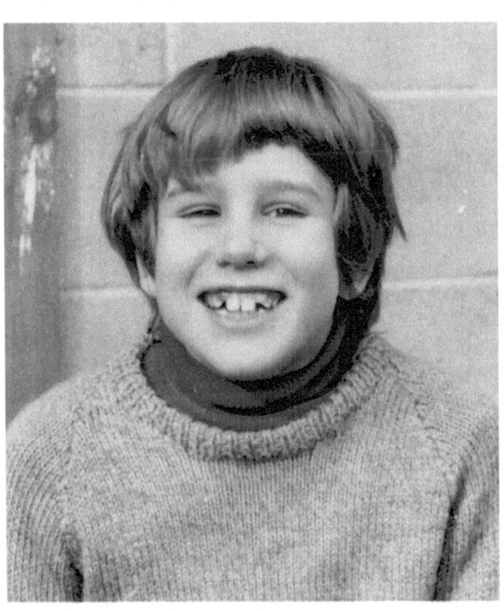

Jeremiah age six

19. THE LONG COMMUTE

It was a pleasant day in June,1974. Jeremiah, age six, played nearby as a New York friend, Katrina, lolled on the couch on the multi-windowed porch of our house in Walden. Renting the house I had grown up in and growing a quarter-acre garden for our own use, Jack and I were homesteading — doing as much as we could to be self-sufficient, which meant growing as much of our food as possible, burning wood for heat, cutting our firewood, making maple syrup, and putting by vegetables and fruit for winter.

We were part of a food-buying scheme, a cooperative purchasing system, whereby households put in orders and congregated on delivery day to break down the 100-pound bags of flour, beans, raisins, nuts, and other items according to each family's orders. Over time Jack and I also purchased two Ashley wood stoves and two sets of cross-country skis, poles, and boots through this same coop. Buying in bulk and in numbers afforded substantial savings.

Everyone had a copy of Stewart Brand's *Whole Earth Catalog*, a counterculture and product publication with the tagline "Access to Tools."*

The Whole Earth Catalog began publishing in 1968 with a focus on self-sufficiency, ecology, alternative education, do-it-yourself practices, and holism. You could order anything from maps, courses, and books, to well-designed tools for gardening and carpentry, to equipment for hiking and pottery making. You could even get chainsaws and early computers from the catalog.

There were lots of potlucks in those days — homesteaders gathering to socialize and share ideas. The delicious meals often included live music, and everyone brought their kids — no sitter needed.

For reasons of his own Jack planted fifty feet of rutabagas every single year. I don't really like those hardy turnips and never served them at home beyond adding a few to a beef stew. But I didn't want them to go to waste and solved the problem by bringing a scalloped dish of them to every potluck we attended. After a while people began asking me for the recipe.

On that balmy day in 1974, I said to Katrina, "I've been thinking I'd like to take a course."

"What kind of course?"

"Something different. Something I don't know much about." I'd been itching to learn something new for some time, though hadn't landed on what it might be.

She nodded. "I'll send you a catalog; I think I know just what you are looking for." She went back to New York, and I forgot about the conversation until in August a thick catalog arrived in the mail from the New School for Social Research in New York. I opened it to a listing for a course on The History and Development of Human Consciousness. I knew immediately it was just the ticket; it was exactly the kind of course I wanted to take. Then I noticed it was taught by someone named Jean Houston — my last name!

Oh, but New York. I could never commute to New York City from here in northern Vermont. I kept coming back to the subject all that day, and by the next morning it came to me that if the course were being taped perhaps I could purchase the tapes. I sent off a letter inquiring about it.

I had errands in Montpelier that day, and stopped to see a friend in Marshfield on my way. She wasn't home, but I went inside to write her a note, and there on her kitchen table was a copy of *Quest* magazine, featuring an article by Jean Houston on the cover. This was a real coincidence. I read the piece, which confirmed my desire to take the course, and by the time I reached home that evening, I had moved from requesting tapes to thinking that if I really wanted to do this, I had to find a way to get myself to New York once a week to take it in person.

I made calls and learned there was one train per day to New York from Montpelier which left at 9:30 p.m. and arrived in Penn Station at 7 the next morning. There was also a train that left New York at 6:30 p.m. and arrived back in Vermont at 7 a.m. Jack wasn't opposed to the idea, but he was a free-lance writer, I was working part-time for a local newspaper, and we simply didn't have the money for it. I asked my friend Claude in upstate New York for a loan, and he sent me $200. It was coming together. Another friend gave me some Valium. I would take a half tab when I got on the train to relax, and I slept like a baby on every trip to the city that entire semester.

Arriving at 7 a.m., I would get breakfast and make my way to the New School, where I'd join some thirty others for the three-hour class. On that first day I scanned the bulletin board in the entrance hall and spied a help-wanted posting by a psychologist seeking someone to transcribe case notes for a book he was writing. I typed my way through the afternoons, and then it was back on Amtrak's *Montrealer* (now known as the *Vermonter*) to Montpelier where my car awaited me in the parking lot.

I was thrilled to be taking the course that I wanted, and by typing through the hours until train time, I was earning the means to keep doing it.

I loved the class. Jean Houston was easily the most engaging and dynamic lecturer I'd ever experienced. She would create spontaneous tableaus, one of which illustrated the winds of change that swept across the

European continent with the advent of the Crusades in the Middle Ages, and led to a new consciousness. She asked two students to stand beside her representing the peasants of that period. She called them *Hans* and *Clothilde*, and described the life they led in a sing-song monotone, evoking the sameness, repetition, and seasonal return experienced in those centuries.

Early in the Crusades people of all strata of society heeded the call to participate in these church-sanctioned, armed pilgrimages to The Holy Land. Some did so for religious salvation, others to meet feudal obligations, still others for fame and fortune. Soon there were successive waves of knights and their retinues journeying to the East, who brought back exciting new ideas and ways of doing things. As Jean told how these wondrous tales of a wider world beyond the manor were filtering back to the *Hanses* and *Clothildes* of that time, their impersonators standing beside her would stop hoeing, stand up straight, and look outward.

The peasants of that era were not unaffected by the new ideas that were heralding an alteration in consciousness. Nor was I unchanged by taking this course. Finding a way to travel to New York and audit the class in person had been a seemingly impossible undertaking at first, given our financial circumstances and where we lived. But I was spurred on by the coincidences—the sheer improbability of Katrina sending me the New School catalog, my opening it to exactly the kind of course I wanted to take, the teacher having my last name, and to top it off discovering an article about her in *Quest* magazine the very next day. It was classic synchronicity—the idea that the coincidence of events in space and time are more than mere chance.

I think a key to my accomplishing this endeavor was my reframing the question; Instead of asking, "Can I do this," I asked, "How can I do this?"

Moreover, in taking the course, not unlike *Clothilde* in the Middle Ages, I was expanding my view of the world, my understanding of history, and of the development of human consciousness.

And though I didn't know it at the time, being introduced to Jean Houston's work would lead seven years later to my taking her three-year Extension of Human Capacities program and gaining an even broader perspective on human consciousness, and human potential.

20. BEYOND BIOFEEDBACK

In the fall of 1976 Jack and I were still homesteading in Walden. The Back-to-the-Land Movement with its culture of grow-your-own-food for greater self-sufficiency continued. I was juggling reporting part-time for a local weekly, harvesting and preserving our quarter-acre garden, helping Jack extract and bottle honey, and working on a children's play.

It was a very inconvenient time to develop a case of bursitis so severe that just raising my right arm was excruciating. If I raised it suddenly without thinking, I would have to huddle immobilized for a few moments until the paroxysm of pain subsided.

I had had bursitis in the past, but never this severe, and it had always gone away in a few weeks. Not this time. However, since my last bout, I had read Elmer and Alyce Green's *Beyond Biofeedback*, in which Elmer described curing his own very severe case of it. His detailed process convinced me to try to alleviate mine.

Green chose a time when he was in a hypnagogic state, which he described as those moments most often occurring between sleep and wakefulness when the mind is awake and conscious, but the body is still in such a relaxed state that the person has virtually no awareness of head, neck, arms, legs, etc. While in this state, Green instructed his body to mobilize whatever chemicals might be needed to dissolve the calcium crystals that lay between the muscle sheaths and were scratching the cushioning pads of the bursa causing them to become irritated and inflamed.* Then he visualized massive infusions of blood and lymph bringing the necessary acids, enzymes or other compounds to his shoulder. He held the imaging for two or three minutes, then monitored for the presence of pain in his shoulder. Finding none and feeling relieved, he fell asleep.

Next morning he was able to raise his hand over his head for the first time in three months. The pain was almost gone. In the following three weeks it faded completely and never returned.

Green suggested a second way of achieving a hypnagogic state might be through a technique that yogi Swami Rama had taught him called "traveling-through-the body." With a wand he would tap certain points, beginning with the spot just above and between the eyes and traveling to the neck, shoulders, elbows, wrists, fingertips and so on through the entire body, instructing the subject to bring consciousness to each of these spots in turn.

I thought this process would be faster for me because I did not often find myself in a hypnagogic state on waking. Swami Rama with his pointer not being present, I memorized the points from the diagram in the Greens' book and, lying flat on my back with my eyes closed, I brought my consciousness to all sixty-one points between forehead and toes and back again. At the end of this exercise I was in a deliciously languid state, and was only vaguely aware of my physical form. My mind, however, was fully alert.

I then instructed my body to mobilize whatever chemicals were needed to dissolve the calcium crystals in my shoulder and to bring forth any acids or enzymes that might be needed to restore the tissues to normal. I did this

*A bursa is a small fluid-filled sac that acts as a lubricated bearing surface for tendons etc.

while lying perfectly still and visualizing massive amounts of blood and lymph coursing through my shoulder, bringing whatever was needed for healing. I soon dozed off.

When I woke a half-hour later I cautiously raised my arm a little. No pain. Had it really worked? I moved my arm about slowly at first, then freely. Still no pain. I hardly dared believe it. The bursitis was completely gone, and it has not returned in the five decades since.

Placebo effect? Perhaps. Or maybe the way the placebo effect works is the body doing unconsciously what I was doing consciously; mobilizing itself to do whatever is necessary to return it to its natural state of health.

In any case, I was thrilled that Green's process had worked for me. Harvesting and provisioning for winter progressed apace that summer, and when a little later *Plays* magazine bought my play I was equally delighted.

21. BUCKING SOCIAL NORMS

Leaving my marriage was the hardest, most painful thing I've ever done. And it took a long time. It wasn't as common in 1977 as it is now. Although a few women who traveled in my circles had divorced, I did not know them well enough to call and talk about it. I think it was so hard because marriage is such a foundational part of the culture. Moreover, no one I knew in my extended family had ever gotten divorced.

We were living at my family homestead in Walden at the time. Jeremiah was nine. It took place about seven years after our communal living ventures and required two forays over a period of some weeks for me to leave and have it stick. I came back after the first time because Jack was in such deep despair that I was truly afraid he might hurt himself. I couldn't bear to think of it. He had been married before and had been the one to leave that marriage. Perhaps the thought of going through the process again was too painful.

After leaving and returning the first time I realized that if I was going to do this I needed to be very clear-headed. I already had a job, but I'd need a car and a place to live. When I left the second time—and stayed left, I had all of these. It had seemed to me irresponsible to choose to leave a marriage that was not cruel or dangerous, and in doing so put myself in need of social services. I felt I needed to be in a position to make it on my own. I had consulted a lawyer and was reasonably sure I could have custody of our son.

I was enamored of another man at the time, but felt that my leaving should not be because of someone else. I needed to make a clean break from my marriage, and if there was to be a liaison with someone else it had to be separate from and occur after I had left the marriage. As it turned out I never did pursue that relationship.

And so, having bought a vintage Chevrolet pick-up truck, found a room to rent in another town within driving distance of my job, I left. The room was beside a waterfall. Whether due to the negative ions said to bring about feelings of well-being, the soothing sounds of the water rushing outside my window, or both, the effect was calming and comforting.

Jere was not with me the short time I was there. Jack never pressed for custody because he thought he had little chance of gaining it, and he soon moved out of the house in Walden. During this period and afterward until graduation from high school, Jeremiah was with one or the other of us. Generally he was with me during the school year and with Jack during vacations. Of course it meant he moved around a lot, but there was no acrimony between Jack and me, and there was full cooperation in working out whom he would be with and when.

Jack and I had taken the usual steps to try to avoid the schism. The psychologist we saw for marriage counseling refused to see me separately. He said that in his experience it was never productive. As a result I never did air all my grievances. I don't know why, but I was unable to do so in our joint sessions. It might have been easier if the counselor had been female.

Early on, I had suggested I might take a sabbatical from the marriage for a finite period of time. Perhaps a year. I felt I needed air, a chance to flex my wings and see what I could do. I didn't have a specific plan, but wanted to break out of the confined existence my life had become. Probably our financial circumstances played a part in this; it was often a struggle to pay our bills, and living so close to the bone, we were limited in the travel and recreational activities we could take part in. At one point it seemed to me that, although not conscious, something in Jack held him back from ever having enough money to be really comfortable. Perhaps it had to do with his parents' struggling when he was growing up. Jack's father, who had perfect pitch, made organ pipes, and there was little call for organs or even repairs during the Great Depression.

Jack had made it clear that moving was no solution to marital tensions because he had tried it in his previous marriage, and it hadn't helped. I wanted to step out of the life I was living with its sameness and predictability and be able to go somewhere else, explore the world. But Jack would have none of it. If you're living apart, you're not together, he said.

I think one of the reasons the separation was such an arduous process was because I was oriented toward supporting or attending to the needs of others, including and maybe especially, Jack, and here I was causing him such anguish by leaving.

Jack came of age in the forties (he was ten years older than I), and his ideas about roles in marriage were pretty entrenched. I, on the other hand, had been a keen participant in a consciousness-raising women's group and wanted to mix the roles up. He'd cook a meal now and then, but he never progressed beyond an attitude of "yes, women have it harder than men, and that's too bad for them, but it's just how it is; I can't do anything about it." While this was one of the issues going back to his never once getting up in the night to attend to a crying baby, it was not the only one. While he espoused support for my participation in the Women's

Movement, he never really changed. Maybe he couldn't. He came of age at the end of World War II and went into the Army right after high school. Maybe I didn't argue enough. After a while it was too late, and I left. A mutual friend of ours once observed that while Jack was a very charming dinner guest, he was not so great as a husband.

I'll own that my inability to fight very well verbally in our frequent arguments resulted in my having resentments which built and built, putting the marriage on a precarious course. I've always admired people who seem to simply open their mouths and intelligible words and ideas come out. Jack, whose parents had come to this country from England after the first world war, was very articulate in the way the English often are. My verbal facility didn't come near to matching his.

Once it was clear we were separating, we had to tell Jeremiah. Jack assured him it was in no way his fault or about anything he had done. Tears began flowing down his cheeks. I ached for him. If this were happening now I would wrap him in my arms and tell him I knew it was hard for him to hear this. I would say that although it was a big change, it was going to be all right, he would be all right, we all would be. But the six-week therapeutic Ark programs in which I was able to process my emotional trauma following my sister's death hadn't happened yet, and I was still frozen in certain situations. Some things are just so hard.

Through all of this, in the back of my mind were two unhappy women that I had known growing up, who had stuck it out, and whose experiences I did not wish to emulate.

One was a neighbor, married to a granite-jawed, iron-willed deacon of the church, whom I saw as long-suffering and subservient to her husband's wishes. As a child, I thought she should just leave and was certain I would have.

I realize now it would have been virtually impossible; she had no skills or money and did not drive. She was stuck.

I had sat at the table with the other woman, also middle-aged, and had seen her be so enraged with her husband that her hands shook. In her case she had a small business and could have left, but I believe that breaking her marriage vows was unthinkable to her. Divorce was exceedingly rare in her day except among celebrities, but from a young age I knew that I would not stay in a marriage if I were as unhappy as she appeared to be.

It wasn't that I hated Jack — I never hated him. He was a good and decent person, navigating life the way he knew to at the time. In the end it came down to my *having* to leave. I reached a point where I knew that if I didn't, I was going to get sick. That, I would not do. I'd had this same "knowing" once before when I was in a dreary, dead-end job. I forget why I resisted leaving it for so long, but after a while my digestive system rebelled. The saying "I can't stomach this" can be literally true. As was the case with that job, after I made the decision to leave the marriage, all symptoms disappeared.

After I left, Jack became deeply involved in the Northeast Organic Farming Association in Vermont. He also played a significant role in facilitating the Farmers Markets that have proliferated around the state, and together with friends formed a men's group. In my view, he became more engaged with life in general.

I do not regret having married Jack. We were very good together for a long time. Perhaps that's just how it is for some of us. It would have been good to keep on together, but we were stuck and for a number of reasons could not seem to get unstuck. We traveled together for a time, and when we no longer "fit," went separate ways.

In the immediate aftermath of leaving I remember feeling like a raw egg — shell-less, without protective covering, and directionless. I had to grow a new skin and find a new identity as I went about maintaining a roof overhead and providing for myself and Jeremiah. Since custody was not an issue, and we were able to work out amicably when Jere would be with him or with me, I never did file for divorce. It didn't seem necessary. It took me ten years to process and come to terms with leaving my marriage.

In those days I often consulted the *I Ching* or *Book of Changes,* an ancient Chinese system based on the concept of synchronicity, the coincidence of events in space and time being more than mere chance.

Having just left Jack, I asked for guidance going forward.* "Mildness in action joined to strength of decision brings good fortune," was the message of the hexagrams I came up with. I understood it as supporting my standing firm regarding the action I had taken and moving forward gently. Which I did. I never considered going back and proceeded to work out a new way of living including an agreeable co-parenting relationship with Jack.

*It was the only time I have ever come up with six changing lines in consulting the I Ching.

22. ONE WITH MY CAR

Most of the experiences I've had that went beyond ordinary sensory knowing have been *in extremis*, or at least have occurred when it mattered quite a lot.

One of those times was in 1988 when I was driving from my home in Walden to visit my sister in West Glover. Soft new flakes were falling on the hard snow-packed road, and three-quarters of the way there I reached a long rather steep hill. I could feel the tires begin to spin and the car start to slow as I reached the steepest part near the top. Uh oh! I did *not* want to have to back down that long hill. I knew that in doing so my car would likely slide backward and then jackknife, sending the rear of my Honda into one of the snowbanks lining the sides of the road. That is, if I were lucky and did not encounter another vehicle laboring up that same incline.

I remembered my friend Elaine telling me about a night when she was a passenger in the backseat of a car that began to buck and then lose power. It was late and they were traveling in a remote area where it would have been hard to get help if the engine died. She said she sat very still and "willed" the automobile to keep going. Slowly it began to regain power and soon was running normally again. They made it to their destination, and she believed it was due to her intense focus on keeping the vehicle moving.

I had nothing to lose and everything to gain by emulating Elaine's example on that snowy day driving to West Glover. I gripped the steering wheel tightly, maintained a steady foot on the gas, and concentrating intensely, *willed* my Honda to keep moving up that hill. I felt one with it in that moment—like my car and I were a single entity. It was as though the rest of the world ceased to exist as my vehicle literally left the ground and bounced forward an inch or more. On landing, I could feel the tires had traction again. Exhaling and maintaining a constant speed so as not to start spinning again, I made my way to the top.

A possible explanation for what happened is "telekinesis" or the ability to move objects with one's mind. To delve further into the physics of this phenomenon, according to Elmer Green in *The Ozawkie Book of the Dead,* all substances have at least a rudimentary level of consciousness and at times may be brought to respond to communication or visualization. Think of Uri Geller bending those forks, think of the Findhorn Community where plant-deva life forces were called upon to grow 200-pound cabbages. There is also the woman in Lawrenceville, Georgia, who lifted a car (likely 2,000 pounds) to free her child pinned beneath it.

I can't say how it happened in my case, and I may never be able to do it again, but in the desperation of that moment I willed my car to do something, and it responded.

23. FELIX IS MY ALLY

Felix and I met at a Carrot Coop harvest party in 1979 in Greensboro Bend. Spirits were high in the upstairs hall where music, dancing, and an abundance of good cheer marked a successful summer of cooperative growing and a bountiful harvest. Though many of us present that night were not growers, everyone in the community was invited to celebrate this brave new enterprise: growing organic carrots.

Felix and I made an instant connection on discovering we both had eleven-year-old boys. We spent the entire evening in conversation. Felix also had a daughter, age ten, and another son, seven.

It was bitterly cold that night—zero or below. The snow crunched loudly as you walked on it, and when it was time for me to leave I was pleased that he offered to accompany me to my truck. But who was this guy? I knew he was an ex-Catholic priest, had lived in South America and Africa, and that he had three kids from a previous marriage. That was all.

Not long after the carrot harvest event, some friends invited me to a dinner party where to my surprise there was Felix again. As before, we hit it off and spent most of the evening talking with each other.

At one point as the party steamed ahead—people talking, laughing, drinking wine, and storytelling by the fireplace—he and I found ourselves in the basement, empty except for a bathtub and a big old Ashley woodstove that supplied the main heat for the house. A register in the kitchen and a large open stairway allowed heat to flow up to the main floor.

There were no chairs in this spacious room, which had a door at one end that opened to a neatly shoveled path to the outhouse and another at the other end, leading to a small root cellar. Not wanting to return to the festivities upstairs just yet, I suggested playfully that we sit in the bathtub. I was tired from standing, and envisioned a restful interlude sitting and chatting companionably in the dry tub, legs dangling over the rim.

He declined graciously. Apparently, he thought I meant sitting, clothes off, in a tub of warm water—I say "apparently" because a few years later when we were living in Southwest Harbor, Maine, he drew a bath one night, and referencing my suggestion at that party in Vermont, invited me to join him in it. He had champagne, soft music playing, and there may have been bubble bath. I was utterly bowled over.

I didn't ask questions, but went with the flow. Feeling some combination of thrill at his gallantry and appreciation for his attention to detail in setting the mood with music and candles, I was swept into the romance of the situation. Felix never failed to surprise me.

At the dinner party in 1979 our hosts' road was not plowed in winter, and it was a half-mile walk over the frozen snow in the moonlight to get to my truck. I readily agreed when he suggested I come with him to where he was house-sitting nearby, saying he would bring me back to get my vintage Dodge pickup in the morning. It was only four or five miles to my house, and I could easily have driven home, but I didn't want the evening to end.

His having set me up to sleep on the couch in the living room, I gratefully gave in to the pull of gravity and the soft support of the sofa while Felix sat on the floor beside it and continued to regale me with tales of his adventures in other parts of the world until, unable to keep my eyes open one second longer, I fell asleep. Next morning he gave me breakfast and duly drove me back to get my vehicle.

He had my attention by this time, but who was he, really? I now knew that he had been a missionary-priest, had ministered to rubber workers in Bolivia, had worked in Tanzania, and more recently had lived in Puerto Rico, Canada, and Ireland where his kids were born, one in each of these countries. And now here he was, with his outsize personality, harvesting carrots in sleepy little Walden where I had grown up. How improbable!

He really was larger than life with his Irish lilt and phrasing, his talk of "clown shows," "cuckoo birds," and use of words like "wee" in place of little. When someone went the extra mile to help others he called it "angel work." He referred to himself as a cuckoo bird, and a gypsy rover. His hearty laugh, and endless supply of stories, memories, and anecdotes from living in so many places were part of him, too. He was also a great listener; his questions made folks feel he really wanted to know them. People used to say that wherever he went he was accepted as a native.

But was his story real? The question kept circling inside my head. Perhaps he was an imposter. I didn't know a single person who had known him prior to his coming to Walden. I had seen the 1961 movie "The Great Imposter," and Felix's life story was every bit as fantastical as the one Tony Curtis portrayed in the title role.

As I was ruminating about the question before going to sleep one night, a voice inside my head said, "Felix is your ally." Since the words had come unbidden, were crystal clear, and contained the word "ally," which I never used in conversation in those days, I was inclined to give it credence. It was as though some entity outside myself was sending me a message.

Felix and my mother

It had been two weeks since the dinner party, and I decided to trust my instincts and pay him a visit. I found the strawberry farm and the tiny one-room cabin that was his lodging in exchange for helping with berries in summer. He was not at home, and I left a note. Next day he came to see me, and for the next twenty years until he died in 1999 we were happily allied.

He soon moved in with me, and his three kids joined us for the summer. I did most of the cooking, and he always did the cleanup afterward. In lieu of saying grace as we sat down for the evening meal, he would kiss the cook — me.

Over time I learned more of Felix's story. He was an ex-priest because the Catholic Church had been more than ready to grant his request for release after he was involved in various activities not to their liking; first in Bolivia and later Stateside. He was "silenced," which meant being sent to a monastery to "relearn institutional obedience." He was, as he said, "de-frocked."

He had certain stars that he lived by. Perhaps as a result of his association with Dorothy Day and her Catholic

Worker Houses of Hospitality at which anyone in need was given food and a place to sleep, he eschewed buying new clothes and found whatever he needed in thrift shops. On principle he vowed never to own property.

Though he drank a lot, he appeared to be able to handle it, and when we were in financial straits when we first moved to Southwest Harbor, he didn't drink at all. He was of rugged build and was thirteen years older than me.

As a Maryknoll missionary priest Felix traveled a circuit by boat to the villages along rivers deep in the Amazon rainforest. He was an excellent swimmer, and more than once risked his life freeing the weed-tangled propeller of his boat in crocodile-infested water.

He knew intimately the lives of his flock. Unlike other priests in the region, he didn't reside at Church headquarters, which offered luxurious comfort. Instead he opted to stay with the villagers where he performed marriages, christenings, baptisms and funerals on his rotational visits. Except for a rare trip home to see family, he lived in the jungle with his charges.

At length he secured a grant to purchase 250,000 acres of rubber tree forest for forming a Cooperative. At *Blanca Flor,* as the plantation was called, he set up schools and invited the natives, who harvested the white latex sap from the trees, to come with their families to live there. The women were busy with their work, but the children were eager to learn everything while the men only wanted to learn arithmetic. They knew they were being cheated when they sold their big rolls of latex to the rubber companies, but, not knowing math, were unable to argue effectively. Felix was a Liberation Theologian before there was a word for it.

Gardens were planted, the men and children were learning, and all was going well until the rubber barons, unhappy at losing tappers to the venture, sent in men with guns who shot two of the harvesters. The Catholic Church, not wanting to be associated with this violence, recalled him to the States, saying he had "gone native."

This was bad enough, but a few years later Felix was asked to accompany the body of a member of the Sugar Cane Brigade, who had accidentally drowned while swimming. The contingent was made up of American college students, who had gone to Cuba to help with the harvest. As a priest, it was thought that Felix's presence would avoid it becoming an international incident, which would have served the political agenda of factions opposed to the Brigade going to Communist Cuba.

It worked. The press was in attendance at debarkation, and the presence of a priest in a white collar accompanying the body dispelled any suggestion that it had been other than an accident.

Sarah and Felix

For the Church, it was the last straw. Unable to countenance one of its own being at the center of yet another newsworthy incident, he was recalled to Rome, where he was divested of clerical office; henceforth he was no longer a priest or a representative of the Catholic Church.

24. SOUTHWEST HARBOR, MAINE

It was 1980. Jeremiah was attending middle school in Vermont and living with Jack. I had visited a private alternative school in Greenwich, Connecticut, which Elaine de Beauporte, my mentor in the Human Capacities program, had been instrumental in creating, and which I thought would have been ideal for Jeremiah — in fact, for any child. The students did not sit in regimented rows of seats, but could sit on the floor, in a window seat, or in a chair, and there was considerable freedom regarding what to study and when. I was also drawn to the Audubon Expedition Institute headquartered in Maine. But living in Greenwich would not have been realistic financially and the Audubon program was for college students.

Since Felix was drawn to living by the ocean where he could fish, we traveled to Maine to investigate schools on the coast. I had spent summers on Nantucket with my sister Sue and family, but Maine was different. I was inspired by Winslow Homer's rugged Maine coast paintings, the state's thriving fishing culture, and swashbuckling sea adventure lore also stirred my imagination. I visited a couple alternative schools south of Rockland, but the tuition was prohibitively high, and the housing in these towns was also beyond my means.

Southwest Harbor, however, held promise. A walk around the pier made it clear it was a thriving fishing village — there were lobster boats and stacks of traps everywhere, and a fish cannery nearby. The public school was not huge and appeared to be a healthy focus in the town. Also, I had come to realize that tuition for any experimental school was likely to be out of my price range.

We rented a cozy house at the edge of a little wood about a five-minute walk from the ocean and set up housekeeping. It had a broad wooden deck with a railing that featured seating with a back. Very inviting. We ate lots of mussels which we foraged among the rocks a few minutes' walk from our wee house. Disdained by the locals as being hard-times-fare from when they'd had to eat them during the Depression years, they were abundant.

Although I had lived in Boston, San Francisco and Los Angeles, this was my first time in a small village right on the water, and I was keen to learn the history and ecology of the place. The sea breeze with its mix of fish, salt, and ocean scents was new to me. I planted a small garden and found the black soil denser than the friable medium I was used to in Vermont, but was able to grow lettuce, radishes, and some greens. I made good use of the local library, carrying home lots of books on the history and background of the area and the state as a whole.

I found people to be welcoming if somewhat reserved. Jeremiah, who entered school in the fall, palled around with another kid new to the school and reached out whenever a new boy moved into the town. Fe and I found jobs packing fish at the cannery. It was piece work and while Felix was quite slow, his jovial manner and abundant cheer won him over to those in charge, who soon found hourly work for him moving crates of sardines and supplies around. I was fast enough, but found my legs got tired standing in one place for long periods, and after a few weeks I left. I later found employment as a nursing assistant at a care home in nearby Bar Harbor.

Come early spring 1981 we were comfortably ensconced in our new lives on the coast of Maine. Once school was out, all four of our children—Jeremiah and Fe's kids Doc, Mosie, and Mehal, ages twelve, twelve, eleven, and eight would be coming for the summer. The way ahead looked smooth and promising—that is, until I discovered that despite using birth control I was pregnant.

What to do? I was working as a nurse's aid at a nursing home in Bar Harbor and Fe was employed at the cannery, but our financial situation was tight.

Also—not that it was an obstacle—Fe and I were not married. In the parlance of the Southwest Harbor fishing community we were "huggers." Not only that, I was not divorced. A friend had told me that after all the struggle and heartache she went through to achieve her divorce, on receiving the cold bureaucratic letter stating it was final, she burst into tears. I was in no hurry to experience something similar, especially since I had no particular reason to do so. Jack and I had figured out how to share custody and we had no contested financial issues.

While we probably could have worked out the details of my getting divorced and Fe and I marrying, financially speaking we were not in a good place to bring a newborn into our lives. Also our kids were on the cusp of being teen-agers, and we had entered a new phase in our lives.

I was not panicked. I gave it serious thought. Fe was on board with whatever I wanted to do. In weighing the question I imagined our lives with and without a new baby, and my way soon became clear; I would seek an abortion. The procedure was not available in Maine in 1981, but it was in Vermont, and I made plans to drive to Vermont and go to the Planned Parenthood Clinic in Burlington.

Meantime, Easter Sunday was upon us, and Fe suggested we take a boat to one of the small islands off Mt. Desert, something he had long wanted to do. Now abandoned, the one he chose had been a thriving fishing community at one time.

It was cool that day, but the brilliant sunshine made the water sparkle and took the edge off the chill. As we walked along the sandy beach, I took off my shoes and walked barefoot. We could look across the cove to a clutch of small cottages that had once housed the fishermen and their families. Painted in deep blues and pastel colors, they were clustered around a smattering of piers that reached like fingers out into the sea.

After a while, Fe having sauntered some distance ahead of me, I mused about my being pregnant and my upcoming trip to Vermont. I had read in Jeannine Parvati's *Hygeia* about a woman, who was pregnant in an untenable situation, had talked to the being growing inside her explaining why she couldn't keep it, and then in the most loving way had asked it to leave. I had done the same, setting aside time to be tender and gentle in the process.

As I walked along the shore, the blue Atlantic lapping at my bare feet, I suddenly felt with a keen certainty that I should submerge in that ice-cold water. I quickly took off all my clothes and stepped into the freezing ocean. I waded to about mid-thigh and plunged in. As soon as every bit of my body was under water including the top of my head, I leapt up not quite stifling a yell and frantically gasped for air. My scalp ached from the cold as I scrambled to dry off as best I could, using my socks for a towel. I pulled my clothes onto my clammy body and hustled to catch up to Fe, who wrapped his arms around me, sharing his warmth. My teeth were chattering uncontrollably, and we left soon afterward.

The following day I had my period. The spirit-entity had left. I was no longer pregnant.

I expressed my gratitude to the soul and to the unfathomable force for good that is in the universe. I didn't talk about this with anyone except Felix — not because it was some dark secret, but because I had no really close friends in the area at the time. Also, I felt closure and rarely thought about it until some forty years later in a conversation about the Supreme Court's decision to overturn Roe v Wade, when I told two close friends. I never regretted my decision to end my pregnancy. It was the right thing to do at that time.

Many years later I offered a sand play session at a fundraiser to support an education program in India. It involved an 18x24x3-inch wooden tray containing sand, and choosing from a variety of miniatures—people, animals, household items, religious symbols, etc.—that a person would place in the tray to make a picture. The subconscious is engaged in choosing the items and placing them in the tray, and the picture that emerges is useful to therapist and client in tracking her progress as they talk about it. In my blurb describing the session I had said that I used it in my therapy practice, and that it was known to be helpful in reconciling opposites and in making decisions.

The woman who purchased the session was in her forties, married and pregnant, and had a seventeen-year-old daughter. In addition, she had a medical condition such that soon she would not be able to bear another child even if she wanted to. She had been struggling for some time over whether to see the pregnancy through or not and sought help in making her decision through doing sand play with me.

Recalling my own dilemma re an unplanned pregnancy some 40 years earlier, I asked the woman to draw a line in the sand dividing the tray into two parts and to find objects portraying her life as she imagined it with the newborn on one side of the divide and to set up the other half as she envisaged her life without it. She became engrossed in creating the latter, and when both parts had been executed, flushed with pleasure, she told me she had her decision; she did not want to continue the pregnancy. She had wonderful plans for the many things she wished to do, and they would not be possible with a new baby. She was very pleased to have resolved her question.

25. GREENS ISLAND BECKONS

After a time working at the fish factory followed by a couple winters as stern hand assisting the skipper on a lobster boat, Felix bought his own craft. His plan was to motor some seventy miles south to Greens Island off Rockland, Maine, where we had friends, and dig clams for the summer. Work boats in this area must be registered and are often named for the skipper's wife, sweetheart or children; Felix called his "The Sarah Lovejoy" after me, which pleased me greatly.

After school was out Jeremiah would be spending the summer with Jack in Vermont, and I planned to join Fe on Greens along with his daughter Mosie, who would be coming up from Mamaroneck, New York. The three of us would spend the summer camping and clamming—all of us in tents and Fe doing most of the clamming.

But a mishap nearly upended our idyllic fantasy before it even began. One morning as Fe set about making final preparations to sail his vessel south, he dropped his keys in the murky water at the pier. Catastrophe! The water was about ten feet deep and this was his only set. In that instant his dream of a summer on Greens Island, which had been so near, was suddenly very far away.

He spent the rest of the day groping around in that cloudy gray seawater with a grappling hook trying to find those elusive keys. He went down again after supper to look some more and at about eight o'clock returned triumphant; against all odds, he had found them. I was amazed and thrilled; I knew how much the venture meant to him. I was especially impressed at his persevering at such a seemingly hopeless task.

Over time I came to see that Felix was undaunted by obstacles that would dissuade most others; he would take on projects that many wouldn't even attempt. When one of his dentures broke in two, he patched it together with a glue he found at the drugstore, and by repeatedly repairing it was able to use it for several more years. When his small inexpensive portable radio gave out he painstakingly took it all apart and got it working again. His can-do attitude and resourcefulness resolved a great many predicaments.

26. EXTENSION OF HUMAN CAPACITIES

It was a mystery to me how a new-age advertising circular containing a brief, fine-print announcement of Jean Houston and Robert Masters' Extension of Human Capacities program found me, but it did. It was 1981, and Felix, Jeremiah, and I were living in Southwest Harbor.

I had commuted from Vermont to New York some eight years prior to audit Houston's History and Development of Human Consciousness course at The New School for Social Research in New York and had found the class exhilarating and richly informative. Eager for more of Jean's creative and dynamic teaching, I set about applying for this new program, and happily, I was accepted.

Jean's current offering was month-long sessions each July for three years. It was based on the premise that most people use only a fraction of their human potential in a world increasingly in need of all the latent capabilities, intelligence, and creative thinking that can be brought to bear. Though not an academic program per se, it could be made the focus of one, and some of the participants chose to do this.

Included in the program were a number of fun practices for extending human capacities developed by Jean and her husband Robert Masters based on the idea that they are latent abilities innate in all of us *Homo sapiens*. These included exercises to enhance the senses, synesthesia for cross-sensing, multitracking or laying down the neural and perceptual basis for becoming more flexible and multifunctional. In an exercise she called "skill rehearsal with a master teacher," we identified an activity we wished to be better at and via guided meditation invoked the presence of a master teacher (real or imaginary). This entity, with words or perhaps feelings or musical sensations, helped each of us to improve a skill. I have since led this exercise in groups and have invariably been surprised and delighted at how very effective it was in helping participants advance their abilities.

These along with Robert's psycho-physical body work and Jean's animating lectures drawing on philosophy, psychology, anthropology, ancient history and religion, all of which were firmly in her wheelhouse, were part of the three-year course of study. Christopher Fry's poem "A Sleep of Prisoners" was a touchstone for the program—especially the last line, "But will you wake for pity's sake?"

As was the case when I took her course at the New School, I didn't have the money, and again asked myself not if, but *how* I could come up with the fee. My solution was to write to some of my sisters and Felix's brother asking for a loan of two hundred dollars from each, which I paid back as soon as I could.

One hundred forty of us, ages twenty-five to eighty-five, gathered at Ramapo College in New Jersey for the first month-long intensive of the three-year program. What a rich learning experience—pleasurable, inspiring and fun! Every day in the vast windowless, womb-like gym we were treated to stirring lectures, moving ritual enactments, exercises for developing and enhancing human capacities, and body work. Threaded through the days were an abundance of high-energy music, dancing and hilarity. Jean, whose comedy-writer dad had written for Bob Hope and George Burns among others, could also be very funny.

We were introduced to the work of Eric Bohm, Ilya Prigogine and other cutting-edge scientists. Therapeia—

the group enactment of stories and myths on the order of ancient Greek theater was always a high point for me. Not unlike the dramas of ancient Greece which have been called a form of storytelling, communal therapy, and ritual reintegration for and by the combat veterans of those times, it was designed for group healing.

One such enactment that we did was centered around a vet in the program, who had served in Viet Nam and was struggling with guilt feelings over having killed people in his role as an Air Force gunner.

We began with a powerful guided meditation invoking a place of oneness in which there was no separation between us who were living and those who have passed on.

At this point Jean asked the ones in the group who identified with the victims of the bombings, to play those roles by lying on the floor. The rest of us were instructed to gather on the other side of a dividing line where we were to represent the "green world" by holding objects from nature or wearing green.

The veteran, Matt, a husky fellow in his forties, was asked to carry each of the eight victims, some of whom were large heavy men, over to the other side. This task took some time, and Matt was sweating profusely when he carried the last body to the green world. At that moment Theophane, another program participant and a Trappist monk, stepped forward, extended his right hand, and said to Matt, "Your sins are many, and they are all forgiven." There was a hushed silence as the sacredness of the moment hung in the air. It was powerful not only for the guilt-besieged airman, who experienced a profound healing, but also for the entire group. I was moved to my core at being present to and a part of this ancient healing practice. These forty years on it is as clear in my memory as though it happened yesterday.

27. TEMESCAL CANYON

In addition to the July intensives, we gathered in January for week-long interim meetups at the Presbyterian Conference Center in Pacific Palisades, California. I almost didn't attend the first gathering in 1983 because I was between jobs and apartments and was wary of incurring the expense. The fact that I decided to go was largely due to a conversation I had with my advisor, Elaine de Beauporte.

When we discussed the question of my going, she asked if I wanted to go. I said, "Yes, of course I *want* to go . . ."

"Then go," she said. "I advise you to go." That settled it. I went, and while the meetup was four days in length, I ended up staying two years.

It is warm in Southern California in January, much warmer than in Vermont, and the Center was just a mile up a slight grade from the Pacific Ocean. I had brought my bathing suit and during a break between lectures and capacity-expanding exercises I went for a swim. The staff in their sweaters and sweatshirts were aghast, but for this Vermonter it was a little bit of heaven. Is it any wonder that at the end of our four-day meetup when manager Tom asked if a couple of us might like to stay on as volunteers, I raised my hand? Why not? I was still between jobs and had nothing pressing to return to.

As a child growing up in Vermont I had often yearned to know what lay beyond the swaths of green mountains stretching out as far as I could see from my spot atop our farm's highest hill. I'd spent a year in San Francisco when I was in my twenties assuaging that childhood longing. Now it was the 1980's, and I was in California again; this time at the Presbyterian Conference Center, a world apart from the clotted urban architecture and tight labor market of San Francisco in 1963.

I gloried in discovering the natural world at the Center — its dry brown summers, balmy winters, the lemon trees growing in people's yards, the stately palms, and especially the beautiful oaks and eucalyptus that grew at the site in Temescal Canyon.

Eager for new adventures, Jeremiah was all for coming west, and joined me at the Center after his freshman year at Hazen Union High School in Hardwick, Vermont. He slid right into being a teen volunteer.

Felix arrived soon afterward, also signing on as a volunteer while he availed himself of some badly needed dental work at UCLA School of Dentistry. By then he and I had evolved a pattern of living a few months together and then being apart for a period of time, always staying closely in touch via letters and phone calls. We hadn't planned it this way, but in order for each of us to follow our interests we needed to be in different places from time to time.

Jeremiah was introduced to an entirely different economic class when he entered Palisades Charter High School for his sophomore year that fall. When he attended a party featuring a live band given by one of his classmates he was ushered in by a butler. For the friend's sixteenth birthday he had been given a shiny new pickup truck so that he could transport his two dirt bikes to distant bike paths.

The homey, no-frills Conference Center with its largely volunteer staff sits cheek by jowl with upscale Pacific Palisades, home to a number of movie stars, the Getty Villa Museum, and The Self-Realization Fellowship Lake Shrine built to honor the major religions and their unifying harmony. While the Getty Villa and the Lake Shrine survived, sadly the high school, the Conference Center, and over 6,000 homes were badly damaged or destroyed in the 2025 Palisades fire.

The director, Tom, was in some ways a kind of latter-day St. Francis. Reportedly, he'd been living the high life—shrewd business dealings, real estate development, and hedonistic living—when inexplicably he began losing the use of his right arm. With the help of a minister, who was a healer, his arm was restored to full function, and he did an about-face and pledged his life to serving the Lord. How better to begin than by helping to resurrect a down-at-the-heels campground newly acquired by the Presbyterian Church?

Much appreciated for his ability to make things happen on the physical plane as well as his sincere desire to do good work, in due course he advanced to being manager. It was referred to as the campground because it had been a family camping area for many years under the aegis of the Methodist Church. Under Tom's direction and with the help of four paid staff and numerous volunteers, it was soon hosting non-profit groups at reasonable rates from all over the country whether or not affiliated with the Presbyterian Church.

For my twenty-five hours per week of volunteer work I mostly helped out in the kitchen, which suited me fine. It was a lively place with other volunteers also assisting Mark, the head cook, who did the menus, ordering, and the bulk of the meal preparation for the groups that came for conferences and retreats. When a short time later there was an opening for assistant cook I was invited to stay on as paid staff.

Soon I was acting as head cook on Mark's days off with the help of one or two volunteers. I found that transitioning from cooking for my family to preparing meals for groups of anywhere from twenty to two hundred was mainly a matter of multiplication; it basically required adjusting the recipes.

I have always liked to cook and had put together a sizable collection of favorites that I could draw on.

The volunteers were mostly men and more than half were African American. One day, diminutive David, a volunteer in his early twenties and a devout Christian, neglected to set the emergency brake in the decrepit station wagon he used for his rounds cleaning cabins. When it began rolling backward he attempted to stop it with his bare hands resulting in his being pinned between the station wagon and one of the dorms. His right hand was injured such that he became eligible for disability benefits and did not do much in the way of work thereafter — a state of affairs, I observed, that suited him just fine. To paraphrase a line in a song by William Cowper, "the Lord works in mysterious ways."

I was fond of Sam, a large, strong, and gentle volunteer from the Mississippi Delta, who would tear up when he told how much he missed his mother. At our Christmas party he blew us away with his beautiful clear tenor rendition of "Silent Night."

There was Boma from Sierra Leone, who fell madly in love with pretty Patty, another volunteer. All was well until Patty began subjecting him to abusive tirades and violent rages. Her behavior, I later came to understand, was symptomatic of borderline personality, a psychiatric disorder in which the object of a person's affections may be showered with sweetness and love only be to be turned on later and reviled — sometimes violently. A broken heart in any setting is painful to witness.

The US government had conducted a number of space missions, and Star Wars movies were playing in theaters at that time. Wayne, a young volunteer who frequently drew kitchen duty, was entranced by these stories and claimed to have been abducted from his cabin, transported in a space ship to a distant planet, and then returned to his dorm. I could see nothing to be gained by arguing with his fantasy.

People were sporadically showing up at the Center in search of a place to crash, and often as not Tom would engage them as volunteers for short or long periods. Though said to have been a tough boss in his previous career as a real estate developer, I observed that he had a soft spot for people in need. I thought at the time there might have been some kind of underground communication system through which these disparate people heard about the Center (I believe I was the only one to come as part of a group). Now I think it more likely they were steered by law enforcement or social service agencies to this church-run retreat center where at a minimum a person could get a meal and a bed for the night.

As a volunteer I was lodged in one of the long, low dorms, each of which contained eight camp beds and nothing else. Who needs bureau drawers when you have seven cots on which to lay out your clothes? Mine were minimal, in any case, since I had packed for just four days. I later bolstered my wardrobe from thrift shops in the area. Eucalyptus seed pods were continually plopping onto the roof of my dorm, and I would gather them up and breathe in the scent. Heavenly!

Once I became a member of the staff, I was given a lovely 1940s-era cabin with a gas fireplace and a tidy little kitchen. Best of all I could literally step out my back door onto a steep trail leading to the top of the mountain behind my house. A two-hour hike along the ridge looped down to a brook — gushing torrent in spring and bone-dry creek bed in mid-summer — that ran along the eucalyptus and oak-lined floor of the canyon back to my house. There were birds and breezes that wafted through the trees in the bright California sunshine. The wild sage, too, was fragrant and pungent. One time when I had started on my two-hour-loop hike too late to avoid the mid-day sun and began to feel dizzy from the heat, I plucked some sage leaves; sniffing them sustained me until I reached home.

One night I heard something outside my cabin and stepped out the back door to investigate. I was transfixed for a moment as I stared into the eyes of a magnificent large grey coyote. I quickly scurried back inside as he, doubtless as surprised as I was, soundlessly disappeared into the dark.

While about a quarter of the parties that came to the Center were church groups on retreat, non-profits such as my Extension of Human Capacities assemblage, were also welcomed. As a staff member I was able to sit in on lectures and seminars by such luminaries as Joseph Campbell. In answer to a question from one of the workshop attendees he said there are two types of people: one that lives as fast and furiously as they can while the other tends to live more moderately saving herself for the long haul. I could see how this benefited the human race evolutionarily speaking and decided that I fit into the latter group.

Another speaker I made sure to catch when I could was Robert Bly. His first workshop, a self-help men's group exploring maturity via the Iron John fable, was closed to non-participants. The following year he came with a troop of writers—right up my alley—but again it was closed. I gleaned what I could from conversations at mealtime, and at the end of their stay I wrote a poem about them which I gave to Bly. I was hoping I might be invited to be part of the grouping that would continue sharing writing after they all went home. He read the poem aloud at lunch, but alas, no such invitation was forthcoming. The following is an excerpt from my "View From the Kitchen" poem:

He's a man of 60 perhaps
    With the face of a child of seven
    Shining as ideas come tumbling forth— Confessional poets,
    The Wild Man and the Wild Woman, Rilke, the
    singing of frogs with rain on your face. . .

In between the sandwiches and homemade soup.
    At night he and his intrepid band troop into the
    womb of a long, yellow dorm
    And in the lateness and lamp-lighted dark
    Stir a great primordial soup
    As they drink their wine and share their poems.
They're heading home now — the poet and his devoted following.
    Leaving some of us wistful in
    their wake.

Near the end of my stay in Temescal Canyon I was introduced to the work of O. Carl Simonton, who with his then wife Stephanie Mathews-Simonton had done pioneering work with cancer patients employing the concept of the mind-body connection.* He regularly brought patients to the Center, employing meditation and mental imagery and instilling the idea that they could have some control over their experience of the disease.

One of his innovative ideas was to invite his patients to experience fire-walking as a way to demonstrate to themselves that a long-held belief might need to be re-examined. At the time, virtually everyone believed that if you had cancer you would die of it. He thought that if his patients found that, contrary to common understanding, they could walk barefooted on live coals without burning their feet, it might open them to questioning their belief that cancer was always terminal.

A 3x9-foot bed of glowing red-hot coals had been prepared for the event in a grassy area away from the buildings. Staff were allowed to witness this phenomenon,

*O. Carl Simonton and Stephanie Mathews-Simonton co-authored *Stress, Psychological Factors, and Cancer* and *Getting Well Again.*

and I watched fascinated as a couple of the patients availed themselves of the opportunity and negotiated the bed of coals unscathed.

The embers were still glowing after Simonton and his patients left, and the expert leading the event invited us staff members to try it. I remember striding around briskly and imagining myself walking across those coals until I had a feeling I could do so safely. At this point I stepped forward and quickly crossed the glowing nine-foot carpet. While I felt warmth around my feet, I detected no sensation that my soles were being burned. What I was most conscious of was the sound — like the swish of tissue paper — as the bottoms of my feet scuffed over those embers. On reaching the end of the strip I inspected my feet. The bottoms of my feet weren't even singed, and there was no redness.

Thinking about it afterward, it seemed to me important that I had taken the time to arrive at the sense I could do this without being burned. Did I enter a state similar to when I dowsed? It didn't feel just like that. Did it have to do with being in a state of heightened adrenaline? I wondered if those Salem women who were burned at the stake as witches could have survived if they had known about this. Probably not, since they were subjected to flames and smoke, not coals. Also, while it seemed to me that I could have maintained my focus and walked a much longer carpet of coals, I was not surrounded by a rowdy mob calling out hurtful words as those women probably were.

While there were many positives that came with working at the Center, there were also conflicts and issues. Though I didn't put it together until afterward, an altercation between the head cook, Mark, and Jim, his assistant, whom I ultimately replaced, almost certainly was due to Manager Tom's assigning Jim to two full weeks as head cook without a break. Tom, at that time, had no appreciation for how hard it was to work in the kitchen for an extended period without a day off. Jim, who had been sober for well over a year and was planning to have his daughter join him in the spring, began unravelling under the strain and went off the wagon. A dispute arose in which he threatened Mark with a butcher knife, and Jim was fired.

It was a tragic situation. I liked Jim and felt badly about taking his job, but was powerless to make things different. Tom, whose earlier life had been primarily concerned with construction and business dealings, still had many rough edges. He simply was not attuned to the demands of cooking for large groups or the nuances of addiction recovery. Over the time I was there I saw many positive changes in him— notably that he became less driven to serve the Lord by making the Conference Center a great success and more cognizant of the physical and emotional lives of members of the staff and himself.

One day while exploring the ridge behind my cabin, an expanse of brown grasses dotted with wild sage and other arid-climate plants, I happened on a small circle of stones. I was entranced. How long had they been there? Decades? Centuries? I sat down at the edge of the circle, and it seemed to me there was a quickening—a rarefied stillness, a sense of sacred space. Who had made it? How was it used? Every year in the fall, two Chumash women from the area came to harvest acorns in the oak grove along the base of the canyon, but they conversed in a native language and never spoke to anyone. I didn't think they were connected to the ring of stones.

Unexpectedly scheduled to cook on my day off one week, I didn't have time to prepare a piece for a television script-writing course I was taking at the University of Southern California. Alas, I fell from grace in the eyes of my instructor, a lovely man in his 70s. I sensed his disappointment in me, but I wasn't about to make excuses. I had a job and it had to be a priority when it conflicted with my other activities.

I hiked up to my sacred circle, slipped into my customary spot at its edge and poured out my distress. While I had friends and family in faraway places, at that time I had no one to talk things out with at the Center. I felt significantly better after doing this, and thereafter whenever life became thick with knotty issues I would go to the circle and, sitting in stillness, express my concerns and questions. I would always receive wise counsel inside my head or find a way to put things in perspective.

28. OUR THOUGHTS AFFECT OTHERS

It was July, 1983, and the second month-long intensive of Jean Houston's Extension of Human Capacities program in Ramapo. Some ninety of us were ranged around the room waiting expectantly for a woman who would be demonstrating how our thoughts affect others. She began by asking for two helpers to join her at the front of the room.

She showed us how to establish "yes" and "no" by asking Bev, the first volunteer, to extend an arm out at shoulder level and while thinking "yes" to resist when Jan, the other helper, laid an arm on Bev's forearm and attempted to push it down. Try as Jan would to force it downward, it held firm.

But when she asked Bev to think "no", and Jan applied pressure on it, she struggled but was unable to hold it at shoulder level. She simply couldn't withstand the downward pressure on her arm, and it dropped to her side. Both helpers were adamant that they had brought their full strength to the exercise.

The workshop leader then asked Sid, another volunteer, to leave the room. At this point we who were watching were asked to think negative, disparaging thoughts about Sid, "what an untrustworthy, sneaky, suspicious guy" he was and the like.

When he returned, not knowing our instructions and Roy, another helper, attempted to push Sid's arm down, it was as though he had no strength to resist; it went down immediately.

The leader asked Sid to leave the room a second time, and this time asked the rest of us to think of him in a very positive way, "what an attractive, intelligent, and all-round good person" he was. When he returned, again not knowing our instructions, his arm held firm when Roy attempted to force it down.

I marveled that our thoughts, positive or negative, could have that much effect on another person. Of course, there was a whole group of us thinking either positively or negatively about Sid; still it made the point that our thoughts about them do affect other people.

My head was abuzz with how we might use this phenomenon. Was there a way it could be used to advance good causes like addressing climate change or effecting peace in war-torn parts of the world? Most significant in the moment was how clearly the exercise showed how our thoughts impact other people and perhaps ourselves. I'm thinking here of times when we engage in negative self-talk or hold self-deprecating thoughts or conversely see ourselves in a positive light—strong and as a force for good.

Another time in the Human Capacities program we watched a video of a mother in a therapy session with her two young sons, one of whom had been isolating and exhibiting depression. His mother did not look at him the entire period —all but ignored him—as he sat silent and downcast. The other boy was smiling and beaming as she looked at him often and with obvious affection as she spoke to the therapist. She and this son also mimicked each other's posture and movements, seemingly unaware they were doing so. It appeared that the child with a problem was not seen or thought of in a positive way by his mother or perhaps in any way at all, while the happy, thriving child received lots of good attention.

Here was another example of positive or negative regard — or perhaps no regard — having an effect on another person.

I resolved that going forward if I caught myself disparaging someone else or myself in my thinking, I would consciously switch gears and look for something positive.

29. A DIFFICULT QUESTION

One question that came up for me after about two years at the Center was whether or not to return East.

After his sophomore year at Pacific Palisades Charter High School, Jeremiah wanted to return to his Vermont high school for his last two years. I was supportive of the idea, and he returned East while I stayed on at the campground. But as he entered his senior year I was faced with the question of whether to stay on or to leave. If I was in California during his senior year in high school I would not be part of decisions about what he would do next. I didn't want to miss this process, and I didn't want him to drift away. It seemed to me that I risked losing my connection with him in that liminal space between graduation from high school and whatever was going to be next for him.

On the other hand, I liked working and living in Pacific Palisades and taking writing courses at USC. I liked the brown grasses in late summer, the pungent scent of bay leaves, the oaks and eucalyptus trees, the mountains with their hiking trails, and having the Pacific Ocean nearby. In short I liked everything about where I was living. Despite occasional conflicts and issues, I felt like I fit.

Moreover, a job had come open with oncologist O. Carl Simonton, who brought a new group of patients and their support persons to the Center for a week each month. I was perfectly aligned with his mind-body-connection approach to working with them. His staff urged me to apply for the job, which entailed being a kind of hostess-den-mother to each new group.

What to do? I was pulled in two directions. After going back and forth about it for several days I decided to bring the question to my stone circle. But before I did this I called my mother. I might have called any number of people, but I think I turned to her knowing half-consciously she would say what she did.

"Well, of course *I* think you should come back . . .", she began. Though she did not articulate it, I knew she was thinking I would be near family again and especially Jeremiah. In any case when I hung up the phone, my way was clear. No more equivocating. When I went to the stone circle I didn't pour out my dilemma, as I had thought I would; instead I expressed gratitude for my decision to leave.

In the days that followed I began packing and putting together a resumé for workshops I hoped to give at Nantucket Island School of Design and the Arts that summer. My sister and family lived on Nantucket, and I knew I could stay with them. I hoped to offer a creative arts training for teachers and parents and to lead a Hero's Journey group for middle-schoolers. I had led a version of the course for children in the Pacific Palisades during my time at the Center based on the theme Joseph Campbell so elegantly describes in his book *The Hero with a Thousand Faces.*

In the months and years that followed I remembered my time in Temescal Canyon with fondness. But that time was over, and I've been firmly planted in the East ever since.

30. FINAL MEETUP

Our final meetup at the Presbyterian Conference Center in January 1985 was a celebration, graduation, and send-off rolled into one. A part of it was a grand Human Capacities Fair in which each of us was to share a talent or project or lead an activity.

I had made several of my poems—most of them the result of experimenting with automatic writing à la William Blake —into a little booklet , which I titled *The Awakening of Diana.* (At the time I was trying on names, one of which was Diana after the Roman goddess of wild animals and the hunt).

Blake's process entailed constructing a poem, not with one's conscious mind, but channeling the words from some external entity. Since I was not privy to any such outside source, I simply allowed the mix of words and images that came to me to float up from my unconscious whereupon I set them down. Following is one of them:

Beasts and wild things jostle in the teaming woods
Quacking ducks stretch and arch their necks
The feathered owl flies soundlessly across the moon
The baby's cry holds back the muffled night.
The frost creeps in on chilly windowpanes
Lazy smoke drifts out the chimney top
The baby moose lowers its homely mouth to drink
The kettle sings atop the kitchen stove.

Where has gone the maid who used to milk the cows?
Are the mufflered, mittened children home from school?
Are there elfin folk in yonder hollow tree?
Does the lassie think she'd like to skip from school?

The winds will blow the rafter beams quite clean
The sound of rain will go on through the night
The opening is difficult to find
You've found it when you're on the other side.

I had made covers for my little books of poetry and tied them with a piece of rawhide and a feather. These I sold at the fair for two dollars.

Cover of my book of poems

One of the participants in the Human Capacities program was 80-year-old psychologist Bill Smukler, whom I had gotten to know over the three years of the program. He had told me about his forty-day training program for therapists and others seeking an in-depth therapeutic experience, which he had dubbed The Ark.

Though it sounded interesting, and I'd often felt frustrated that I could bring little more than a sympathetic ear to the often emotionally troubled volunteers at the Center, I didn't consider Bill's six-week event for myself because I couldn't have afforded the fee.

Notwithstanding, at the end of the last session on the very last day Bill came walking across the lecture room to ask if I'd be interested in coming on the Ark in January as the cook. He said I'd have an assistant and could participate in group therapy sessions, dream clinic every morning, and sand play as much as my schedule would allow. I didn't hesitate; I said yes.

When I learned later that a cook had already been hired for the program, whom Bill then had to "unhire," I wondered if his wanting me in that job might have had something to do with my poems. He had bought one of my booklets, and perhaps he thought I might benefit from the Ark's in-depth psychological program—which I certainly did.

I think it was likely a combination of the psychologist in him seeing the above, the rave reviews for my cooking skills during the weeklong meetups at the Center, and the Army-sergeant-leader part of him sensing that my positive energy and Human Capacities experience would be a boon in his Ark program. I have always liked to cook and had created delicious menus taking care to honor any special dietary needs in the group.

One year, on the last day of a week-long January meetup, as I bowed to applause expressing appreciation for the meals, I was suddenly scooped up by five or six of the participants and carried face up around the dining room. It caught me entirely off guard, and I suppose the sheer incongruity of finding myself five feet off the ground amid loud clapping and cheering made it extra thrilling. I had seen this kind of thing before, but had never imagined being celebrated in this way myself.

I had been in communication with Nantucket School of Design and the Arts prior to the meetup and was slated to lead a Hero's Journey group for nine-to-twelve-year-old children that summer. Now I had work in a fun, therapeutic setting for January and February as well. My life was re-forming and, though I didn't know it at the time, was moving in a new direction.

As I flew home in June, somewhere between the Rockies and New York I felt a change in my body—a very subtle contraction. I reflected how very different the West Coast was from the East; the West with its easy living, wide-openness to new ideas, and endless sunshine (you could plan a wedding on any given day in summer and be assured it would not rain). The East Coast—at least the New England and Vermont that I knew—promised cold winters that advised planning for heating fuel, putting up produce from the garden, and outfitting your car with winter tires. Moreover, your vehicle would not last as long as it would in other parts of the country due to rust from the salt applied to roads in winter. There are other differences, too; you are more reliant on your neighbor in the East for social life, exchanging information, or help getting your car out of a snowbank. You become constitutionally adapted to a culture, history, and way of life quite different from that in the West.

Sarah at Final Meetup

31. THE ARK

It was 1986. The location was a large two-story house in Pennsylvania's beautiful Lehigh Valley in the foothills of the Poconos. I had been hired to cook for the twenty-five or so staff and participants who made up the Ark, a forty-day residential training program for therapists and others seeking an in-depth psychological healing experience.

Metaphorically based on the biblical story, it was the brainchild of psychologist Bill Smukler, who saw it as a personal journey where one might face one's deepest psychological issues in a nurturing and protected space away from the cares of daily life. Participants were exposed to a wide range of therapeutic modalities including dreamwork, gestalt, sand play, art, primal, Jungian and many different talk therapies. To reinforce the idea of an ocean journey, participants were asked to refrain from contact with families at home except in an emergency.

Bill knew from his Army experience that the Officer's Training Corps was forty days in length. Also that Christ spent forty days and nights wandering in the wilderness, and that other persons of note have spent extended periods alone in the mountains or desert. While the Ark was an intensive group experience, it was isolated from the world at large, and he deemed it long enough for a person to go deep and make significant changes.

There is something to this time factor. I found that I could hold a sense of a week or even a month, but after that, awash in a heightened psychic state as we all were, I began to lose all sense of time. By the fifth and sixth weeks I had no feel for how long we had been together. Weeks? Months? More than a year? In the charged, deeply-engaged medium we were immersed in it began to feel to me as though we had always been there.

Bill's parents had suffered under pogroms in Russia, and after his mother died, Bill, age five, together with his father and two brothers, came to this country to live with an older brother. When Al and his wife had company Bill's father would be banished to the basement because he spoke no English, ran a fish store, and was obviously a foreigner. The five-year-old, feeling compassion for him, would always stay down there with him until the guests had left.

While small in size — a Jewish leprechaun if there is such a thing — and mild in manner, the adult Bill was outsize in wisdom, organizational ability and sheer grit. He also had a playfulness about him and a keen sense of humor. He told about being in a training seminar in Italy during WWII when the instructor accidentally knocked a live grenade onto the floor. The other G.I.s froze, but Bill quickly picked up the grenade and tossed it out the window. It turned out it was not live, but was a test. His quick thinking paid off, and he was promoted to Sergeant.

Ark programs were offered every two years through 2000, and once I had experienced the magic, the time out of time, the pure unadulterated fun as well as profound inner work, I was hooked; I never missed a single one and participated in eight Arks. That first year I was the cook, the following year I was a trainee as participants were called, and after that was one of the leaders. Trainees, given psychological tests before and after the forty days, showed an average of two years' psychological growth.

Leaders' responsibilities included meeting daily with the other staff to review trainee progress. There was also planning for the opening ceremony, an elaborate affair in which the entire group sat in a circle, each person with a stuffed version of their power animal and a candle. One-by-one they ritually expressed their goal in coming on the Ark. Later at the closing ceremony each one would tell what she or he had gained over the forty days.

Each of the leaders also served as a support person—someone they could always go to with problems or for comfort—for one or two trainees. One of my jobs was collecting people's peak experiences and reading them to the entire group at the final ceremony. I enjoyed doing this because I always had a number of these epiphanies myself and knew how special it was for trainees to be reminded of theirs in the ritual.

The Ark was a microcosm, a compressed time experience in which a person could return to major childhood traumas, this time with awareness and loving support, and find healing. Many of the Arkites adopted "good mothers" during their time there as a way of remedying the experience they'd had with the mother they had growing up. Adopting a surrogate mother was not a rational process, but was something that seemed to happen on an intuitive level. One year, after I had taken on a leadership role, I was adopted as a good mother by five of the trainees. This meant that one or another would seek me out for snuggling at evening story time, come to me for comfort in a group therapy session, or ask me to be their support during a staged psychodrama in which they confronted a perpetrator from their early life.

At "town meeting" each morning everyone in the Ark community gathered to learn what would be happening in the day ahead. It might be a ritual funeral for someone dealing with unresolved grief over an abortion, the ceremonial transfer of Bill's leadership role as the "Noah" of the Ark to another staff member for the ensuing week, or announcement of the seminar to be given that day. Everyone — leaders and trainees alike — was asked to bring something to share with the group. One year I gave a talk on writing as a means of personal growth. Another time I offered a presentation on identifying one's support system on returning home from the Ark, which in addition to certain friends or family members, might include a yoga or tai chi course, a pet, or a group that was meaningful.

One of the presentations given by a trainee that stood out for me was titled "What Myth Are You Living?" Another one, "Facing Your Shadow," was followed by a party that evening. It is difficult and sometimes unpleasant to identify and face the parts of oneself that are deemed unattractive or unacceptable and that tend to be relegated to the unconscious. To reinforce their awareness of this elusive aspect of their make-up, staff and trainees came to the evening event dressed as their shadow selves. One person came dressed as a vamp complete with low-cut evening dress, cigarette holder and false eyelashes. At Bill's suggestion I dressed one side of myself in male attire such as my father wore and the other half in a housedress and apron suggesting my mother. All evening I alternated between hailing folks in a confident deep-voiced manner emulating my dad, and speaking in a quiet voice and adopting a retiring manner like my mom. It was an informative experience.

The daily morning meeting was also the place to air any problems or grievances that might have cropped up during the previous 24 hours — anything from "someone's snoring keeps me awake" (trainees slept in a large third floor room called the nursery) to a plumbing problem in the second-floor bathroom. As time went on I found I could intuit when a trainee was in need of support and would offer him or her a backrub as we all sat through the announcements and discussion.

Sand play was a major activity at the Ark.* The three-inch-deep trays containing sand that were used rested on waist-high supports. At any time of day or night a trainee or staff person could trek down to the sand play room in the basement and make a sandbox. The walls of the room were lined with shelves containing groups of miniatures—dragons and scary pieces, religious symbols, people of all ages, animals, houses, objects from nature, and all manner of means of transportation. Not unlike dreams, the pictures that people created in their sand trays using these tiny objects reflected what was going on in their psyches, and when shared in a quiet, respectful exchange with a staff member, often led to new insights for the trainee and information about her therapeutic progress for the therapist. It was an especially powerful adjunct to the other therapies employed on the Ark.

Also located in the basement was the "shadow room," a space with mattresses and padded walls where a trainee might "demolish" a childhood perpetrator by repeatedly bashing pillows with a plastic bat or yelling at top volume at someone they had been wronged by.

Many different therapeutic styles were employed on the Ark including primal integration therapy in which one could get in touch with traumatic incidents from childhood and re-enact and express the emotional hurt, anger, fear,

---

*It originated with Dr. Margaret Lowenfeld, who developed a therapeutic process for use with children involving miniatures and a tray of wet or dry sand. Psychologist Dora Kalff studied with Lowenfeld and later with Carl Jung, who, following his break with Freud, had found it healing to create little towns in the sand on the shores of Lake Zurich. Kalff developed a sand play process, which combined Lowenfeld's World Technique with Jungian psychology and Tibetan Buddhist principles of engaged witnessing.

loneliness — whatever it was — in safety and with support. It allowed for discharging the trauma they had been carrying, perhaps unconsciously, in their bodies for years because it had not been safe to do so at the time of the event.

An important aspect of this work was discussing the process after the session with the attending counselor (therapists operated on a rotating basis) and perhaps investigating how the trauma had led to life patterns that were limiting as well as how the person might have more behavioral choices going forward.

I found primal work especially effective in dealing with my anger and grief over coming home from school at age ten to find my dog Ricky had been "put to sleep." It was something I had shut out of my memory for the many decades since it had occurred. Because it rose to consciousness in the context of talking about my sister's death when I was seven, I was able to express my feelings about both losses.

After I had dealt with these traumatic incidents in a few sessions, I was able to access emotions that had previously been blocked. For the first time, I was able to feel sadness when parting from people I had grown close to. Doing this kind of work, I was told, often results in neural reprogramming and our being able to experience more at both ends of the spectrum of pain and pleasure.

The one-on-one and group therapy sessions, dream clinic, seminars, and chores (there was a work wheel designating trainees to vacuum common areas, clean bathrooms, set-up the dining room for meals, etc., on a rotating basis), were interspersed with music, singing, and dancing and, of course, meals and a bedtime story at night. This last provided participants an opportunity to snuggle in a puppy pile while one of the leaders read stories from children's books. Over the six weeks many of the trainees would regress to a child state, and this was a welcome activity. I loved being part of the snuggling heap as a trainee and later as a leader reading the story.

Shortly before the end of the forty days, the entire group of trainees and staff were treated to dinner at a nice restaurant in nearby Jim Thorpe (named for the famed Native American athlete). The purpose was to help participants begin the process of integrating back into the larger society. Following is a poem I wrote and shared with the group on the day we made the trek off the premises in 1990:

The Ark is time out of time — a tiny bubble in the ocean of the universe — a kind of Raggedy Ann and Andy world where adults are turned back into children, dragons are slain and windmills are tilted.

It is tea parties and sand play and schedules and meetings and chores after breakfast and affectionate greetings.

It is ritual killings, funerals and deaths, babies and births, bottles and breasts.

It's sand play and horseplay and trying on names. It's Dudley our dog and poems and songs.

It's our shadow-selves come out for one night. It's lost socks and laundry, hollering, insight.

It's sweet friendships, good mothers and good daddies too, and enough stuffed animals to make up a zoo.

It's weeping and laughing and raging and playing; it's living our stories and collecting wise sayings.

The Ark is now over, yet will never be done. I wish you all ice cream and feelings and fun.

You've loved and you've hated and called to your mother. As we go out into the world let us help one another.

Since a great many of the trainees became significantly regressed over the six weeks of the program, beginning to reintegrate before reengaging with the outer world was an important step. It only took people so far, however. Very shortly after the Ark on which I was a trainee, I remember being in a supermarket with other Arkites and, on a lark, climbing into a grocery cart to be pushed around the store. It was not something I had done before or even on a lark will likely do again.

I had had a couple of brief therapeutic experiences over the years, which were helpful for getting through crises, but they were nothing like the forty-day immersive milieu of the Ark. I found the therapeutic process fascinating and engaging. I know that not everyone finds it so compelling or even seeks it for personal growth or making changes, but for me it fit like a glove. Hence, when the time came to take a serious look at how I would support myself long term, I chose therapy work because of my time on the Arks. I went back to school at age sixty-eight for a degree in Counseling Psychology.

I now know from personal experience as well as from observing others that therapy can be life-changing. We Arkites held a celebration-of-life ceremony following Bill Smukler's death in 1999. When it came my turn to speak I said that because of Bill and his Ark programs "I was not who I would've been, but instead am who I could've been." The self-understanding and tools for dealing with issues as they come up as well as the neural reprogramming from doing primal work have meant I am able to "feel" more and function better and consequently live a fuller, happier life.

Bill Smukler

32. DOWSING MY WAY HOME

The first time I reached beyond what I knew I could do was at a weekend workshop at the Craftsbury Outdoor Center in Vermont's Northeast Kingdom.

It was a glorious warm day in autumn, and following the introductory talk when the rest of the group trooped off to the dining hall for supper, I opted to go for a walk. I knew from having skied at the Center that it boasted a vast network of trails angling off in different directions. Happy to have some quiet time, I delighted in the brightly-colored leaves as I set forth. I was aware of various signs and arrows at the many trail junctures, but paid no attention. Unless you have a map by which to orient yourself, how are they useful? Besides I knew these trails, having traversed them on skis many times.

At length, though I was enjoying the balmy air and the woody-sweet scent of the leaves, it was time to return to the Center for the evening program. I remembered the two turns I'd just taken, but at the third fork as I headed back I was unsure. Tentatively, I ventured right. In the midst of several acres of maple trees with no buildings or rocks or other identifying markers, how does a person figure out where they are standing?

I tried to get my bearings from what I remembered of the terrain and followed a trail that sloped downward toward the sports complex — or so I hoped. But no, a short time later it climbed upward again. I was flummoxed. I kept walking, but it was sinking in that I was lost — thoroughly and utterly lost with little hope of happening on the sequence of trails that would lead me back to the Center. Moreover, I noted with some uneasiness that the shadows were lengthening, and in a few hours it would be dark. If I couldn't find my way back I'd not only miss the evening program, I could very well be in these woods all night. I took small comfort in thinking that at least I wouldn't freeze. I'd be cold all right in my cotton shirt and jeans, but it wouldn't drop below freezing, not in September.

At this point it occurred to me to try dowsing—not the usual way with a forked stick or a pendulum, neither of which I had with me, but through tuning in to body-knowing. I'd had some success finding underground water lines using a forked cherry whip, beginning when I was a child. Years later as a reporter for *The Hardwick Gazette*, I covered The American Society of Dowsers conventions, which were then held in Danville, Vermont. Its headquarters is there today.

At these conventions dowsing was used for many different purposes from illness diagnosis and facilitating healing to finding lost objects. Driving home from an evening talk, after spending two hours in a room packed with veteran dowsers, I recall my body feeling super charged—tingly all over. I think I'd taken on the vibrational level of the professional dowsers seated all around me.

One instructor had told us we didn't really need a dowsing stick, wand or pendulum; that we could find things by simply tuning in with our bodies. I went home and tried it to no avail. But now, lost in the woods at the Outdoor Center and feeling a little desperate, it occurred to me to try again.

I decided my car might be a stronger target to focus on than the cluster of buildings that made up the Center campus. At the next diverging trail I closed my eyes, focused intently, and mentally asked which way to my car, all the while slowly turning around in place. When I felt a subtle but unmistakable pulling sensation in my forehead I opened my eyes and found I was facing a trail. Encouraged, I began to follow it. I repeated the exercise at the next trail juncture and at a number of different forks and trail crossings after that, receiving and following the same sensation in my forehead each time.

Some forty minutes later *tada!* I was back at my car at the Center. Hallelujah! I felt great affection for my old Honda Civic at that moment.

I was glad I hadn't missed the evening program, greatly relieved not to be spending the night in the woods, and elated that my dowsing skills had worked. I'd gone beyond what I'd ever done and had gotten "unlost."

There are different theories about how dowsing works, one of which holds that it's the magnetic pull of the water vein or whatever you're dowsing for, that causes the stick to point down or the pendulum to circle rapidly. The one I subscribe to says it's the energy field around the human body responding to the signal of the dowsed object; i.e. we pick up "electromagnetic emissions" through some sensory system other than the five senses we habitually use. I've heard it said that just about everything is knowable if we can formulate the right yes-or-no question and can tune in finely enough to pick up the signal.

33. REMEDY FOR A RUNNY NOSE

On a cold overcast day in January 2008 when even the birds stayed huddled out of the wind, I was in Charlotte, Vermont, for a League of Vermont Writers workshop. The imposing brick building I found my way to was the venue for a training on using a new app for writers. This aid was said to facilitate keeping track of notes, chapters, characters, time-lines, etc., when working on novels and other longer-form writing. I might not have gone except that I knew the tool was quite complex, and I wanted the help learning to use it that I knew I could get in a small workshop. To top it off, this would be the last time this subject would be offered by the League.

But I was coming off a miserable cold, and though I was past the apex of it and feeling fine, I had moved on to non-stop mucous drainage; my nose ran constantly and copiously.

What to do? I just needed something to check my nasal flow. Desperately I searched my medicine cupboard. I tend toward herbs and home remedies more than over-the-counter stuff, but nothing looked promising on either count.

In Stone-Age times and on through the Middle Ages, how did people come to know which were the medicinal herbs and which ones to use for specific maladies? Many herbaceous plants used in ancient times are used today either in lab-prepared modern medicines such digitalis, a heart medicine derived from foxglove, or straight up in tisanes, decoctions, tinctures or infusions such as raspberry leaf tea for menstrual cramps and strengthening bones, and crushed jewelweed leaves to bring relief from poison ivy.

Herbalists and healers may have stumbled on some of these treatments and antidotes accidentally, I surmised, while others perhaps intuited them. It is said that we modern *Homo sapiens* have lost many of our ways of knowing, but I thought that if I concentrated I might come up with something helpful. Worth a try.

I focused my attention as I looked over the spices and condiments scattered among the baking powder, salt, cornstarch, and cocoa in my kitchen cupboard until I came to dulse. Hmm. Might an infusion made from this dried seaweed help my mucous issue? Something about it being a product of the sea made it seem more promising than any of the other items. I didn't dowse it; I had a feeling it would work and brewed a cup. Hooray, it did! My nasal drip was assuaged in just minutes.

I made up a large thermos of it, and headed off to my workshop. Throughout the afternoon whenever I felt the need—about every forty minutes—I sipped some of my seaweed brew.

I got the info I was after from the workshop—or rather enough to know that the app was not for me. It would neither justify the cost nor the time it would require to set it up and learn it. But more importantly, the antidote was a success; I did not cause the others attending the workshop distress by constantly blowing my nose, and I now have a remedy for a runny nose.

34. A DOWSING OF CONSEQUENCE

For twelve years beginning in 1988 I worked as a counselor at a half-way house, a group home for young adults transitioning to independent living after having been hospitalized for psychiatric conditions. While in this job I had occasion to use my dowsing skills in one especially consequential situation.

With the help of elaborate supports, the residents of this household were in various stages of learning to manage psychological and addiction challenges enroute to living independently. As a group they mirrored society at large; funny, talented, deceptive, angry, loud, charming, loving.

In my role as Leisure Group Guide on Saturdays I would take small groups on recreational outings. What we could do was wide open within the confines of a small budget. Naturally I chose activities I would enjoy as well as ones I thought these young folks would like. At different times I took them to various Vermont attractions — the Old Growth Forest in Marshfield, roller skating at the rink in Barre, and overnight camping in Groton State Park — two of us counselors leading that trip.

Once I took a small group to Nichols Ledge in Woodbury. Never again! I got rubber legs as my charges trotted to the very edge of the cliff, a four-hundred-foot vertical drop to the pond below. My insistent demand that they *come back from the edge of the cliff!* fell on deaf ears. I couldn't wait to get them off that ledge and down the hill to the car again.

Another leisure activity I never repeated was a trip to Bread & Puppet Resurrection Circus in Glover.* Though not in recent times, I had been to many of the troupe's spectacular performances over the years, always having a great time.

Bread and Puppet Theater moved to Vermont in the 70s and over the years developed elaborate outdoor pageants, featuring enormous puppets—some as tall as fifteen feet. Picture a vast allegorical drama with a cast of more than a hundred volunteers on a twenty-acre stage of rolling hills and forest.

On the beautiful sunny day in 1996, when we set out for our leisure group outing, we had sandwiches, drinks, and chips to munch on. I was eager to share this festive event with the four young men who had opted to come on this trip.

Though I hadn't been for a few years, I was used to parking in one of the little fields near the circus amphitheater, and was disconcerted when we were ushered off Route 16 to park in a vast complex of fields before even reaching the dirt road into the Bread and Puppet farm. We were directed to a spot in the midst of acres of vehicles. I cautioned the guys with me to take note of where we were parked, counting rows and pointing out landmarks in the event that, God forbid, we got separated.

We trekked a long way through the parking fields, which morphed into a camping area—dozens of tents, colorfully

---

*Bread and Puppet Theater began as a small group working to advance its political philosophy and social commentary through art and community in Greenwich Village. They shared fresh-made bread and art, which they maintained "should be as basic as bread to life." Their performances featured puppet dramas, colorful posters, and flags from their inception.

decorated VW buses, and makeshift campers beside little campfires around which small groups were cooking, eating, playing music, and hanging out. The air was thick with the smell of marijuana. Not the best for those in my group with addictions, I thought, as I guided them quickly through the fumes and on to the concession area through which we also had to walk to get to the circus. I knew three of my charges well, and felt I could count on their behavior. The fourth was a recent arrival at the group home and an unknown quantity, but he was quiet, appeared to be tractable, and he wanted to come so I had said yes.

The concessions were another eye-popping change from the last time I had attended the circus. In my prior experience, aside from founder Peter Schumann's delicious, crusty sourdough rye bread, which was free, people had brought their own food — picnics. But here were giant food trucks selling Domino's pizza, canopied booths offering elaborate vegan fare, venues displaying colorful tie-dyed apparel and jewelry, and a stunning array of exotic smoking paraphernalia alongside tables offering prayer beads and mystical Eastern literature.

I remember thinking that those venues had little connection with the circus or the philosophy of Bread and Puppet Theater, and that even if they'd wanted to, the vendors couldn't leave their wares unattended to see the show.

I learned some time later that a post on the internet had touted Bread and Puppet Circus as one of the ten best partying events in the country, and that when the Grateful Dead stopped touring after Jerry Garcia died, the Deadheads descended on Bread and Puppet en masse. But I didn't know it at the time. In any case, the friendly Bread and Puppet Resurrection Circus I had known of yore, "held together with papier mâchè, burlap, twine and staples," had grown from an event drawing crowds of a few thousand to attracting a whopping thirty thousand!*

On we trudged through the steady stream of walkers and jostling knots of people on the final lap of our trek to the amphitheater. At last we arrived at the enormous grassy, semicircular sidehill facing the performance area. Hooray!

I scanned the slope for a spot large enough to put down a blanket and seat the five of us. At length I spotted one that, though tight, would have to do. We had no sooner settled ourselves than the new fellow announced he was claustrophobic and simply could not abide being closely surrounded by all these people.

Nothing for it, I had to accommodate him. Flags that said LOVE, ART, BREAD, etc., were displayed at intervals around the rim of the seating area, and I located one that said PEACE near a tall arching light about thirty feet straight up the hill from our blanket. I was not comfortable dividing my group, but there wasn't room for five of us anywhere along the upper perimeter. I gave the guy a sandwich and settled him under the light post and PEACE flag with the stern admonition that he not move from the spot until we collected him at the end of the show. He solemnly agreed. Back with the others, I glanced up from time to time to reassure myself that he was there.

The show began with human puppets dressed as washerwomen in print housedresses and aprons and workmen in gray shirts and pants converging on the grassy

---

*At its apex the annual Circus was drawing some 30,000 people and had become too big for the town and for Bread and Puppet itself. It downsized, and now stages smaller weekend performances in summer while its colorful bus and puppeteers often appear in local parades. The troupe also tours domestically and abroad.

stage from all directions. Their enormous gray papier-mâchè faces looked worried and careworn as they randomly appeared from the top of the hill and surrounding fields.

I don't know what the guys with me thought as they took in this spectacle.

Not a very talkative bunch in the best of times, there was not a peep from any one of them in response to this opening and the subsequent skits and shenanigans accompanied by the music of the eclectic Bread and Puppet band, I realized that, in this instance at least, what was fun and exciting for me might appear simply strange or bizarre to them.

At the end of the show the giant blonde Mother Earth puppet was paraded forth on tall stilts amid a joyous cacophony of horns, flutes, and drums, signaling the triumph of good over evil. The entire hillside erupted in a standing ovation. This was followed by a flurry of people gathering up blankets, food, and babies and surging en masse up the hill. It was a few minutes before we were able to struggle through the chaos to the PEACE sign to pick up the new fellow, only to find that he wasn't there. He was nowhere in sight. I looked around as best I could amid the surging masses of humanity, but he was not to be found.

Perhaps he had tired of waiting and gone back to the car, I thought. It took us a long time to make our way through the throngs of people coming and going, the food trucks and hawkers of exotic goods, the campfires in the marijuana zone, and the rows on rows of cars to our station wagon, only to find he was not there either.

This was worrisome. I unlocked the car and admonished the other three not to leave it under any circumstances, while I went back for the new fellow; a quest that was aspirational at best. As I considered my chances of finding him, my concerns mounted. I couldn't go back without him—I was responsible for these guys. I *had* to find him. Moreover, in a few hours it would be dark. Should I call the police? In my imagination I saw blaring bullhorns and giant search lights piercing the night sky as they combed the Circus area. But in this multitude how could they find him any more than I could? I doubted they would even attempt such a long shot.

I went back to the PEACE sign, and, of course, he wasn't there. As I began retracing my route to the car, people coming and going ten-deep on either side of me, I realized I could be three feet from him and not see him.

On the verge of panic now, it occurred to me to try what had worked some years before when I was lost in the woods. I closed my eyes, pictured the new guy, and focusing intently while slowly turning in place, I asked which direction would lead me to him. As had happened at the Craftsbury Outdoor Center, at a certain point I felt a pulling sensation, something akin to a subliminal buzzing in my forehead. I opened my eyes, walked straight in that direction for about ten feet, and there he was — the elusive late addition to the residential program where I worked. Hallelujah!

Unperturbed, he said he'd gone to the car and not finding us there had come back to look for us. We returned to the station wagon where the others were waiting. Once we were at the group home again, I reported another successful Leisure Group outing. Ha! And all was well.

I've been told that dowsing works best in situations like this where a lot is at stake. In the years since, I haven't dowsed for anything nearly as consequential. I'm not superstitious, but I read about a man who was able to cure a serious skin condition for people by invoking dowsing energy. After experts told him it just wasn't possible, try as he would he was never able to cure anyone again. I didn't want to jinx my chances of getting out of another serious jam by attempting complicated dowsing situations and finding I couldn't make it work.

Sister Sue at her vegetable stand on Natucket

35. ROSEMARY

During my summer stays over the years with my sister Sue and family on Nantucket I had become acquainted with two artists, both named Barbara. One year they enlisted my services to care for their friend Rosemary, who had stomach cancer that had progressed to a point where she needed someone to be with her at all times.

Since I had worked as an aide in a nursing home at one time, I felt up to the task and comfortable with the responsibility. It was an easy job; I kept tabs on her vital signs, soothed her by applying warm cloths to her forehead, and contacted medical personnel when she needed to go for routine procedures. Another woman came in to make meals and clean.

Rosemary and I got on well. She shared bits and pieces about her life and I was a good listener. I was not intrusive and generally was able to intuit what would make her comfortable. Her needs were minimal early on, but I was available if she needed something,

I found her fascinating. Attractive, in her 60s, she had been something of a belle in her day. Married twice, most recently to a senator, she told me that while she would marry again if she wanted to, she really had no desire to do so. She asked me to always wash her face with upward strokes so as to counter gravity. Given how ill she was, I marveled that she held to her beauty regimen so firmly. I guess one's life-long habits do not simply go away regardless of the circumstances.

One morning when I went into her room to check on her I knew immediately from the rattly sound of her breathing that she was very ill—perhaps dying. I called the EMTs to bring her to the hospital. Later that day medical staff called to tell me she had died. Though not unexpected it was nonetheless a shock, and I was sad.

While my work there was done and my job was essentially over, I had some packing up to do and decided to stay the night. In addition to my clothes and personal items, I needed to pack up the sand play items I had brought thinking that making a sandbox might be something Rosemary would find engaging. But alas, she was too sick even to enjoy being read to.

I went to bed that evening at my usual time, but later that night a strange thing happened; the door, which I had closed and latched when I turned in, became unlatched with a loud metallic *click*. I woke with a start. I was alone in the house and felt very vulnerable. My heart pounding, I watched my bedroom door slowly swing open. My scalp prickled. There was no one there, yet I had the distinct impression that someone *was* there. Rosemary or some version of her, I felt certain, was standing in the doorway looking at me. Was she questioning why I was still there? There was no sound.

Thoroughly alarmed, I clutched the covers up around my neck and waited wide awake until morning. Promptly at seven I called my brother-in-law Steve to come and pick me up. I couldn't get away from that house fast enough.

I can't say just why I was so unnerved by sensing her presence. I had had strange encounters with spirit-like phenomena before and had not been the least bit uncomfortable. One of those times was in 1980 when I was between jobs in Southwest Harbor and spent a couple of weeks with my friends, the Murphys, in Boston. Jeremiah was living with Jack in Greensboro, there was no bus service from Vermont across to Maine, and I had arranged for him to come by bus to visit me in Boston over his spring break. He'd drunk a Coke on the bus ride down and left the red can in my room when he went back to Vermont.

On a few occasions I had felt the Murphys' house shudder despite it being perfectly calm outside. When it shook like this it was not due to earthquakes because no one else in the house felt it. I knew that the presence of water underneath a building can cause strange phenomena at times and assumed that the building shaking was related to an underground spring or water vein. Then I noticed that it seemed to respond to my thoughts about it. If I said to myself, "This is silly, I'm going to ignore it," it would immediately shudder again. If I theorized it might be some kind of disembodied spirit energy, it was still. And so when I began to hear Jere's red Coke can randomly make a sound as though someone had snapped a coin against the bottom of it, I was primed for thinking it was a strange-entity phenomenon. I also wondered if my being in a somewhat unsettled place emotionally might be causing these strange occurrences. I was concerned about Jere, missed him, and also was between jobs in Southwest Harbor. However, after I returned to Maine, leaving that Coke can behind, and found a job working as an assistant at a nursing home, I experienced no further such episodes. The following spring Jeremiah came to Southwest Harbor to join Felix and me and attend junior high school in the fall. I was quite content, and there were no more strange occurrences.

When the Coke incident occurred in Boston I had not been awakened in the middle of the night nor was I alone in the house as was the case when Rosemary died. Also, in the Nantucket instance I was certain the spirit-energy was Rosemary, who had been alive that very morning. Perhaps my fear was linked to my still being there after my job was essentially ended.

The way I understand it now, having read more of Elmer Green's work, is that she was temporarily in a state termed the "after-death bardo," meaning that although she had died and left her body, her astral body or soul had not yet moved on. Perhaps she was just looking to see if I was still there. As for my fear and discomfort, I think it probably had to do with my being alone in the house, and the immediacy of Rosemary having died just that morning,.

36. A CALL FROM MY MOM

It was December 2009. I was driving with my mother to a family dinner at my sister's house in Glover when I lost control of my car on the icy road and hit a tree. The wind was blowing very hard and the compacted snow on the dirt road was very slippery. I had maintained a steady speed in order to make it up the long hill, and as I reached the crest I eased off the gas. It must have been just that much colder and the wind blowing that much harder on the open plateau because a strong gust spun my Camry around so that I faced back the way I had come. My vehicle was off the road and no longer drivable, the left fender having bashed into a maple tree.

My mother said she wasn't hurt. I limped a little, but it was nothing serious, and I headed to the house across the road to put in a call to my brother-in-law to come and pick us up and to AAA to come and tow my car.

Next day, my mother "hurt all over" and went to the hospital where they found she had walking pneumonia, a condition she may have had for some time, and two broken ribs. I suppose it was inflammation around the broken ribs that made it so arduous for her to get enough breath to speak. Four days later, after visits from all of her seven children, she died. She was ninety-two.

Some nine months afterward I heard the telephone ring very early one morning. It woke me up. The ringing must have been in a dream because there was no one there when

I picked up the phone, and it did not ring again. I hopped back into bed and, wide awake, I felt my mother's presence right there in the room with me. I couldn't see her, but knew she was a little to my left and facing me. She didn't speak in words, but in the silent way some creatures seem to transfer thoughts (a friend of mine, who swam with the dolphins in Puget Sound, had told me she received communications from them in this way), my mom let me know that everything was good and that she was perfectly fine.

I felt her presence before me very clearly; it was unquestionably her, and it was clear that she was there to tell me this. I did feel some comfort that she was fine, but I didn't think about it beyond that it was so like her to make sure I knew it and wouldn't worry. While the crash certainly was regrettable, and I wished fervently that it hadn't happened, I did not feel guilty about it because it so clearly had been an accident. Also, while it shortened my mother's life, I knew that her day-to-day existence had increasingly become an effort as she aged. I felt awe at the call in my dream to wake me up and then her presence in the room letting me know she was okay. This was not something I'd ever experienced before.

I saw a therapist several months after the accident to sort through a swarm of complicated feelings, chief among them the fact that I had held my mother emotionally at arm's length for most of my adult life while at the same time being deeply appreciative of her goodness, her wisdom, and that she was such a good mother to all of us. I can't really explain why I had felt the distancing, but at the end of several sessions it had vanished, and I felt emotionally close to her in the way I had as a child.

In all my seven plus decades she had always been there. Now that she was gone I felt bereft. Before she died I don't think I could have resolved my distancing from her, but in sorting through all the pieces over the weeks that I saw a therapist, I was able to put myself back together. This I did by exploring the vivid dreams I had every single week.

When I told my sister Sue about "the call," she said, "Well, if she calls again tell her I said hi."

37. WAKEUP CALL

It may be that something on the order of my back "setback" in 2019 had to happen, that a reset was needed. Perhaps the youthful being dancing on the surface of herself that I was, had to be brought up short in order to ground and inhabit myself on a deeper level.

Some people may get cancer (this happened to a friend), others have a motor vehicle accident (another friend). In both cases something happened that dropped them into a more profound experience of themselves. In my case it was my fragile bones giving way — agonizingly.

Does it help to think that if only I had sold that firewood I wouldn't have been moving it, and it wouldn't have caused me such grief? Not really. The incident — the spinal fracture I sustained in relocating the wood — caused me to stop utterly and completely and take stock of where I was and what was important to me. I was in bed for what seemed like weeks, unable to navigate without a lot of pain.

This break followed two prior incidents, which,, though quite painful, hadn't compromised my activity nearly as much nor for so long, and I hadn't realized there had been fractures from them. They only came to light with my 2019 X-rays. Likely my recent ordeal moving wood had aggravated those old fissures as well as creating a new one.

The event has caused me to take steps to lessen my osteoporosis as well as to maintain awareness of my fragile bones in determining how vigorously to engage in certain activities.

I have always had compassion for others with physical issues, but since my recent mishap I identify with them viscerally as well as emotionally. Also, I am more aware that sometime in the next decade or two, I'll likely check out. I'm not afraid to die and in fact have had a day now and then when I looked forward to "the long sleep."

As a result of my traumatic event I am planning to sort and dispose of a lot of stuff, and I'm being more realistic about what I have the strength and stamina to do. Also I am more particular about how I choose to spend my time. Generally speaking, I am more accepting that there are limits to what I can do and how I can live.

Was there an easier, more gradual way to slow down and get here? Probably. But I don't think the steaming-ahead, obliviously-reveling-in-physical activity person that I was, could have gotten to the more thoughtful, accepting one I am now without a dramatic event — a wakeup call — to bring me up short and lead me to re-evaluate how I live.

38. BRINGING IT HOME

Jeremiah and I lived in Hardwick during his senior year at Hazen Union High School. We were housesitting for one of my aunts who was spending the winter in Florida.

The following year Jeremiah left for Boston to follow his interest in cooking, and I returned to the family homestead in Walden. I found work at a home for young adults with psychological challenges. My good friends and fellow counselors at the halfway house, Allison and Michela, soon joined me as did Felix's daughter Mosie.

I have a special relationship with her — more kindred spirit than kin. From the first year that she and her brothers spent the summer with Felix and me, she appeared to thrive on country living. After other vacations with us in Walden as well as in Maine, at times accompanied by her brothers, she decided to transfer from State University of New York to Vermont's Johnson College and commute from my home in Walden.

Meantime, Felix returned to his beloved Ireland. The folks in Teelin, where he had lived in the 60s and where his youngest child Mehal was born, welcomed him with open arms and soon found housing and employment for him. The plan had been for me to join him there, but when I visited I found that finding work would have been problematic and that it was very much a man's world at that time. I let go of plans to live there, but we stayed connected with letters and phone calls, and over the next decade Mosie and I made a number of trips to see him, often together.

In 1999, ill with lung cancer, Felix let me know that "the train was at the station." I flew to Ireland and was with him in the hospital in Donegal when he died. Though he had never feared or dreaded dying and we had known for some time that the end was coming, it was nevertheless a momentous and sad occasion for me. I was glad I could be with him, and later reflected how fortunate we were to have had two decades together.

Interwoven through all this was my participation in eight 40-day Arks. At the one in 2000, I participated in a session of Grof Breathwork developed by Stanislav Grof and his wife Christina.* In my memory the process involved a combination of deep and rapid breathing and evocative music, which led to hallucinatory scenes—mind movies, really.

Felix had died a couple of months prior to that Ark, and after experiencing a series of images congruent with Carlos Casteneda's *The Teachings of Don Juan*, which I had been reading, the music changed and Felix appeared on my mind screen—a jocular, leprechaun-like version of himself. Sitting cross-legged, he proceeded to banter with me in the lighthearted manner I knew so well. I don't remember what he said, but as a result of this session I felt a wonderful completion. It was as though I had undergone a grieving process of a year or more in that hour and a half session, and I was at peace. I still missed him of course, but I had moved on from the shock of his not being alive and the deep sadness I had been feeling.

*LSD was outlawed in this country in the late 60s, and the couple created a technique for achieving non-ordinary states of consciousness without the use of LSD, providing a legal way for the scientist to continue his research in healing and consciousness.

In due course I went back to school for a degree in Mental Health Counseling. and worked as a counselor at Wellspring in Hardwick for the next fifteen years. Two of the modalities I liked especially were sand play, which I had learned in the Ark program, and leading therapeutic writing groups which enabled me to combine my two principal interests.

These days I enjoy my garden and living where I grew up. I had created an apartment in my house in 2010, and in 2019, Jeremiah, Stateside for good after four years teaching in China, moved into it. His move, occurring just six months before Covid shook the world, might have been difficult had he not left that country when he did. It has been a mutually agreeable arrangement where we often host dinners for each other.

Somehow, when I wasn't looking I have become older than anyone else in my family and in fact older than just about everyone I know except for a few high school classmates and members of my square dance group. Sometimes I'm sixteen and still in high school, or I'm in Boston in my thirties with a new baby, or I'm camping on Greens Island in 1981. I certainly don't feel old.

I continue to use my sixth sense when I need to know what is causing distress in my body or how much of a supplement to take

I no longer take any drugs for osteoporosis. Since dowsing will only give me yes-or-no answers, the challenge is to formulate the right questions. For example, when I asked if there was something I could do or take so that my arms would no longer hurt (a side effect from having taken Alendronate), the answer came back "yes." I then asked if it was something I needed to eat or drink. "No." I guessed at possible therapies that I might try, including acupuncture, which brought up an affirmative. Bingo, I had something to try, and yes, it was successful. After a few treatments I was able to move my arms freely without pain.

When I stand back and look at what I have written, I can see how early on I sought to reach beyond my beginnings in rural Vermont and find ways to experience more of the wider world. When my "Call to Adventure" à la Campbell's *The Hero with the Thousand Faces* came, I answered it, and with the help of allies found a way to commute to New York to take a course in The History and Development of Human Consciousness. Doing this affirmed my sense of agency and introduced me to new ideas and people and ways of understanding.

Ultimately it led to my taking Jean Houston's three-year Extension of Human Capacities course of study, which offered a vast smorgasbord of knowledge, people, and experiences, not least of which was living in community on the west coast for two years. Through this program I met Bill Smukler, which led to my participating in eight forty-day Arks. The wider world of psychotherapy that I encountered in these biennial events brought many new skills and enabled me to deal with the loss of my sister when I was a child.

All of this took place against the backdrop of my domestic life and being a mother, and often using my sixth sense to navigate.

In writing this I am able to see the shape of my life—to see it as the story of my becoming and moving into greater fullness of being, and, ultimately, just as occurs in a hero's journey, bringing it all back home.

Acknowledgements

A book is invariably the work of many hands beyond those of the author. For all the generous and unstinting help I have received in putting this book together I am profoundly grateful.

Special thanks go to Allison Mann and Maggie McGuire for their whole-hearted support for this project from the beginning and for their tireless help in bringing it the last mile.

I deeply appreciate the care and suggestions of my readers Mary Young, Mosie Hill, and Jeremiah Cook and the members of my writers' group: Cindy Bogard, Cynthia Ross, Judith Hinds, Justine O'Keefe, Lyn Kasvinsky, Maggie Thompson, Steve Reynes, Ben Williams, Ron Thompson, and Terra Trevor, who helped me shape it and offered innumerable thoughts and ideas that made it better.

Big thanks go to Judith Hinds for her cheerful help and expertise with line-editing and to Marian Willmott, who magically pulled the entire book together.

Lastly I'd like to thank my high school English, French, and Latin teacher Mrs. (Leone) Cobb (1896-1989), for her personal encouragement of me and many, many others, and whose dedication to teaching meant putting her own writing on hold until after a while it was too late.